Giuseppe Terragni:
his war, his end

Valerio Paolo Mosco
edited by Attilio Terragni

T0351610

This work would not have been possible without the support of Michele Canepa, who generously financed the Terragni Archives.

Editorial project
Forma Edizioni srl
Firenze, Italia
redazione@formaedizioni.it
www.formaedizioni.it

Editorial Director
Laura Andreini

Editorial staff
Maria Giulia Caliri
Livia D'Aliasi
Andrea Benelli

Graphic design
Laura Maltinti

Translations
Katy Hannan

Photolitography
Fulvio Gallotti
Vincenzo Lapiccirella

Photographic credits
Photos on pages 14 and 30:
With kind permission of CE·S·A·R -
Centro Studi Architettura Razionalista
and Flavio Mangione, Luca Ribichini and
Attilio Terragni (published in *Terragni e Roma*, prospettive edizioni, Rome, 2015).
All other photos with kind permission
of the Terragni/Como Archives.

First edition: October 2020

"...a new world seemed to reveal itself in our febrile imagination".

Giuseppe Terragni, Russian Front, 1942

Certain stories remain forever relevant. They refer to those individuals who have been able to create something that cannot be replaced or replicated, and thus, they leave a mark on their era. They are vital witnesses of their times, an important means for understanding the past and the territory of our origins. Some of these individuals identify with their era so deeply, that they absorb their experiences, while others are crushed by them and even succumb and die with them. This is the case of Giuseppe Terragni, the most talented among the Italian Rationalists: an artist who was unique, able to transform the language of Le Corbusier and Mies van der Rohe into an abstract form able to touch the threshold of transcendence. The years that separate us from the events described in this book are long gone, but when events are experienced by an artist, the space of time is magically compressed. Their experiences become our own because, as Benedetto Croce wrote, poets reveal ourselves to us, and this revelation continues to exist beyond time.

Giuseppe Terragni was called up for military service in 1939, a year before Italy entered the war. For a long period, he performed his military duty at the barracks while working on his projects in Como at the same time. His projects involved the controversies which had plagued Modern architecture in Italy since its very beginnings. In the spring of 1941 he left for Yugoslavia and then for the Russian campaign. His letters and photos during this period show he did not abandon his research: he studied the vast steppes for new means of expression, a new spiritual sense for his abstractionism. During his first winter in Russia, he was very active, even combative, but as the situation deteriorated, he became depressed. With the defeat, it became unbearable. The unusual dialectic balance of his personality combined exuberance with private intimate feelings, the avant-garde with the metaphysical, and urbanity with his personal convictions. When confronted with the intolerable prospects of defeat, all this was shattered. He was sent home in a mentally fragile condition after the second catastrophic Battle of the Don. He returned ravaged by a sense of guilt but, as Alberto Sartoris stated, also "spiritualized". In fact, only a few days before his death, around which there is still a certain ambiguity, he designed an epitaph for the future, and his last project: a plan for a cathedral. An amazing project for its mystical influence. It heralded a period of architecture that was never to occur because of the disappearance of one of its most talented exponents. In 1926, the Gruppo 7 wrote their Manifesto, the first document to launch the period of Italian Rationalism. With the other members, Terragni wrote: "We wish to belong uniquely, exclusively, and literally to our own time".

And so it happened. Terragni died on the very day Rome was bombed and a week before the meeting of the Grand Council that was to dictate the fall of Mussolini. His death coincided with the death of an era. The events described in this book resemble those of a Greek tragedy. A battle between an individual and destiny, or in other words, history – a conflict in which inevitably, the individual must yield.

But the hero crushed by destiny, moved by blind forces far more powerful than he, is granted a consolatory way out. He is transfigured by what Nietzsche called the "great pain" in form, in a work of art. We are now in a historic moment which we could define as 'later Postmodernism'. After decades of devaluation and eradication, tragedy has been replaced by cheap masks that purge all that embodies the strength needed to transcend certain events. Captain Terragni's final years are proof of an inflexible truth: architectural forms are not merely external. They do not belong only to urbanity and communication, but, as Terragni's friend Franco Ciliberti stated: "they allow the original essence of life to filter through, and in doing so, save the world from the mediocrity that generally surrounds us".

In writing this book, I was able to consult material in the Terragni Archives in Como, directed by my friend Attilio Terragni, to whom I send my heartfelt thanks. I also had access to countless publications that have appeared over the years, listed in the footnotes, and without which this book would never have seen the light. These include the book edited by Giorgio Ciucci for the large exhibition in Milan dedicated to Terragni at the Triennale di Milano in 1996. In particular, also presented is the fine work by Emilia Terragni, as well as the extensive research on Terragni by his friend Luca Lanini. I would also like to thank Flavio Mangione, Luca Ribichini and Attilio Terragni for the illustrations of Terragni's Roman project reconstructions. My thanks also to Paolo Bercah for his excellent suggestions.

"[...] now that I have clarified the story of Terragni as an architect, only his psychological portrait remains to be completed".

1. Comment made by Zevi in the 1980s to Attilio Terragni, the great nephew of Giuseppe Terragni and editor of this book.

2. The first to suggest a complete analysis of Terragni's work, was his brother Attilio, an engineer, who had been in contact with Bruno Zevi on this subject around 1953; this occurred four years after the exhibition dedicated to Terragni in Como, curated by Mario Labò and inaugurated by Le Corbusier. Labò also edited the extensive review of Terragni's work in March 1963 for *Architectural Design*. Zevi's activity began in 1950 with a chapter on Terragni in his *Storia dell'architettura moderna*, Giulio Einaudi editore, Turin, 1950 (*The Modern Language of Architecture*, Seattle, University of Washington Press, 1978) and continued in 1968 with a monographic issue of the magazine he directed (*L'Architettura. Cronache e storia*, XV, n. 153, July 1968) followed by the monograph published by Zanichelli in 1980.

3. Zevi took part in the Littoriali Games in 1937 in Naples, and again the following year in Rome (pre-Littoriali) and in Palermo. In his book he recalled: "…paradoxically, the Littoriali games were 'the annual meeting of anti-Fascist youth'". Bruno Zevi, *Zevi su Zevi*, Marsilio Editori, Venice p. 193.

This was written by Bruno Zevi following his long research work dedicated to the most talented Italian architect of the last century.[1] In fact, it was Zevi who rediscovered Terragni after the war. This Jewish architectural critic, forced to flee to the United States, was the first to understand that the impulsive, disdainful Fascist architect from Como had been one of the most important figures of the Modernist Movement. Already in the 1950s, he understood that the indefinable, elusive and concise architecture designed by Terragni was one of the few examples that could be used as a reference to regenerate an architectural language which was sliding into a prose becoming increasingly more superficial.[2] Zevi also saw another aspect in Terragni: the affliction of a nation, its mistakes and its defeat, through the testimony of a very renowned Italian whose tragedy was to have been part of the generation that followed the crippling First World War. A generation exposed to the military interventionist rhetoric rekindled after the Great War, from the myth of the "mutilated victory" and the contradictory phenomenon of Fascism. Zevi was born fourteen years after Terragni but also experienced the contradictions present in Terragni's youth. He himself remembered participating as a student in what would then become the breeding ground of the Italian post-war ruling classes, the (GUF) or Fascist University Groups, a participation that, as often occurred in his career, signified excellence.[3] Zevi seemed to see in Terragni his own same mistakes induced by history, and by which, willingly or not, we are all influenced. Their personalities were also similar. Both proclaimed explicit, incisive ideas; both shared the same passion for getting straight to the point and were attracted to swift, decisive, unequivocal action, a behavioural inclination also influenced by the historical situation, a paradigm caused by the specifically Italian phenomenon that was Futurism.

If any distance existed between the two, it was precisely on the subject of architecture. Let us consider Zevi. In 1948, five years after Terragni's death, Zevi returned from the United

States to a liberated Italy, bringing with him a manuscript that was later published by Einaudi, in which he declared his passion for Modernism, which in Italy was exemplified by three figures he admired, and who had died shortly before: Persico, Pagano and Terragni.[4] The title of the manuscript that the young Zevi brought with him his emblematic: *Towards an Organic Architecture*. In his book, Zevi predicted the arrival of an architecture that would be able to manifest the same impetus towards the freedom the author had discovered for himself through the writings of Benedetto Croce and had seen embodied in the architecture of Frank Lloyd Wright. Therefore, what Zevi desired for Italy was the advent of an architecture contrary to the Fascist rhetorical style, an architecture that began with the internal space and symbolically expressed its yearning for freedom through its external aspect. This was what Zevi hoped for in the new Italy: challenging architecture, orographical, not at all representative, openly anti-monumental, using exposed natural materials, able to finally re-establish the distance between the erudite and common language that Francesco De Sanctis was the first to have considered as Italy's greatest affliction. In short, the architecture that Zevi aspired to was a style contrary to the abstract, cold, elitist and intangible architecture of which Terragni was the maximum exponent, not only in Italy. So, in order to promote the organic architecture that he himself had formulated, theoretically, Zevi should have been a harsh critic of Terragni's work, or should have at least kept his distance. But, on the contrary, in the early 1950s, with the wounds of war still open, Zevi praised Terragni, declaring him as an international master of Rationalism. And he was the first to do so.[5] The decision to praise a potential adversary, was a noble, chivalrous gesture, worthy of Zevi at his best. If we visit what is still the home of the Terragni family in Como, in the elegant secluded via Indipendenza, on the outer side of the garden wall that shelters a small patio overlooked by the family home and the professional studio, is a steel plaque: "Where Giuseppe Terragni (1904-1943) lived architecture as a prophecy. On the XXV anniversary of his disappearance". The plaque was created by Giò Pomodoro, a sculptor famous in the 1960s, and was donated by Zevi himself in 1968, the year he organised an important convention on Terragni. 'Architecture as a prophecy' is an expression that recalls the famous conference held in 1935 by Edoardo Persico, entitled "Prophesy of Architecture".[6]

4. Bruno Zevi, *Verso un'architettura organica*, Giulio Einaudi editore, Turin, first edition, 1945. *Towards an Organic Architecture*, Faber; first edition, 1950.

5. In fact, in 1950, Zevi was the first to dedicate a whole chapter of his *Storia dell'architettura moderna* (Zevi, Bruno (1978) *The Modern Language of Architecture*, Seattle: University of Washington Press) published by Einaudi: the book enjoyed considerable international success, and was translated into several languages, placing Terragni among the limited group of Modernist masters.

6. Conference held by Edoardo Persico on January 21, 1935, in Turin, at the 'Società Pro Cultura Femminile' of the Fascist Institute of Culture, published in *Edoardo Persico. Scritti di architettura (1927-1935)*, edited by Giulia Veronesi, Vallecchi editore, Florence, 1968, pp. 117-126. To understand Persico's complex story, it is worth reading the short novel concerning his mysterious disappearance by Andrea Camilleri, *Dentro il labirinto*, Skira, Milan, 2012.

In what was to be one of his last public appearances, a few months before his untimely death, Persico had summarised his school of thought with an idealistic project to place "Human experience in the mirror of Plastic Values". Zevi wanted to recover this project and in doing so, cited Terragni as an example. For this reason he organised the convention, and the following year, in 1969, he edited a monographic issue of his magazine *L'architettura. Cronache e storia* dedicated to Terragni.[7] The cover is poignant: entirely white, without illustrations, and written in large classical style script: "Homage to Terragni". It is poignant, not so much for the title, but rather for the layout of the title. It is divided into three lines: Omagg-Io a Te-rragni. (A play on words of 'Me to You'). Me to you. Me: Jewish refugee, the prophet-champion of organic, material, anti-representative architecture… to you: Fascist, Catholic, the master of abstract, immaterial, representative architecture. Me to you: my adversary, my brother. The huge event that separated the two men was the war; for one, a war experienced as a mission for a regime in which he believed, for the other, a war endured, forced to flee to another continent from where he witnessed the defeat and humiliation of a country that had believed in his same grievances. Me to you. My brother, with whom I share the same grim burden of intellectual honesty.

On September 5th 1939, Lieutenant Giuseppe Terragni, born in 1904, thirty-five years of age, was called up to serve in the army. The Second World War had begun four days before with Nazi Germany's invasion of Poland. Italy entered the war the year after Terragni's call-up in June 1940 with timing that does no honour to our country. In fact, it declared war on a defeated France four days before the Nazi troops entered Paris. It entered the war to share the spoils and to benefit from an alliance that had been originally feared, and even opposed by some, yet later, it was not only accepted but even acclaimed. Terragni left on the same day that the director of the Brera Academy, Rino Valdameri, informed him of the approval of his project for the Danteum: a project proposed by Valdameri himself. The Danteum was a monumental building to celebrate Dante, and was to be erected on the new via dell'Impero opposite the Basilica of Maxentius, postponed to a date to be established.[8] Unfortunate news for Terragni since it arrived at a moment when great changes were underway

7. *L'Architettura. Cronache e storia*, XV, n. 153, July 1968, monographic issue, edited by Bruno Zevi.

8. Luigi Zuccoli, *Quindici anni di vita e di lavoro con l'amico e maestro architetto Giuseppe Terragni*, edited by Luca Lanini, Libria edizioni, Melfi, 2015, p. 150. Accurate information about the event was provided by Giorgio Ciucci. The project of the Danteum did not stop completely after this news. In December 1939, Valdameri worked to obtain permission for Terragni to make further ammendments to his plans in view of a meeting with the Duce, that Valdameri, Senator Alessandro Poss and Vittorio Cini, had managed to arrange for February. During the meeting, it was decided to include the project in the E42 Universal Exposition, a choice that would have necessarily included the involvement of Piacentini. After the meeting, Valdameri asked the architects to make some changes to the main facade, and this all occurred around April 1940. (Giorgio Ciucci, "Terragni e l'architettura" in *Giuseppe Terragni. Opera completa*, edited by Giorgio Ciucci, Electa, 1996, p. 70). Later, according to Paolo Nicoloso, the project was assumed singly by Pietro Lingeri who created a model. Lingeri himself wrote to Terragni in July 1940 to reassure him that he did not intend to make any changes to the design they had agreed together. Paolo Nicoloso, *Lingeri e Terragni* in *Pietro Lingeri*, edited by Chiara Baglione and Elisabetta Susani, Electa, Milan, 2004, p. 68.

OMAGG
IOATE
RRAGNI

153

L'architettura
CRONACHE E STORIA

€ 20,00

Mancosu
editore

1

in the organisation of his work studio. He left home with the grade of Lieutenant in the Third Artillery Regiment of the Army Corps stationed in Cremona and in Caprino Veronese, where he remained throughout the following year, performing his military duties and meantime requesting leave to continue with the work left on his desk in Como.[9] Zevi wrote: "he left without fanfare".[10] In fact, there are no documents, letters, or evidence that bear witness to an event that seems to have been experienced with discretion and perhaps with optimism considering the fact that Italy, which had not yet entered the war, was watching amazed, as its ally conquered the adversary alone. Terragni left for the army when other architects, of the same age, and supporters of Italian Rationalism, remained at home and continued to work, engaging more closely with Rome – the centre of Fascist power – where the assignments were being shared out for the Universal Exposition to be held in Rome in 1942. Como is a good distance from Rome, and although Terragni had designed some remarkable buildings for Como, he had never obtained a commission in Rome and had not won any competitions. His talent was recognised and sometimes even praised, but it was in the general interest that Terragni remain confined to Como, at most, accepting private commissions in Milan, and it was better to stay away from the capital, especially after 1935, when a swerve towards Imperial Classical architecture did not seem to leave much room for his Rationalist inflexibility.[11] And yet, around the time he left for the army, Terragni's ambitions were directed specifically towards Rome.

In fact, news arrived from Rome concerning some cracks in Piacentini's academic front line. Three months before he was called up, in June 1939, Terragni wrote to Mario Cereghini: "We need to set up an architectural studio in Rome. Time to move!". A new studio with Cereghini and Alberto Sartoris with whom he was collaborating in a much stronger way. A new studio with very specific aims: to create great buildings in Rome free of the Piacentino Imperial style.[12] In the meantime there were plenty of commissions in Como. The project for the Casa del Fascio in Lissone, designed with Antonio Carminati, was nearing completion.

It was not a very complex project and the final work details were easily managed without the presence of the architect. However, it was a different case for the social housing project in via Anzani in Como, a project as a result of another, also designed with Alberto Sartoris.

9. Terragni spent a long period in the army before leaving for Yugoslavia (April 1941) in different barracks in Cremona, Ferrara, Caprino Veronese, Schio, Lonigo and Nettunia. On his return from Yugoslavia in May 1941, he went to Cremona, from where he was sent to Russia with the first contingents of the Italian Expeditionary Corps (CSIR).

10. *L'Architettura. Cronache e storia* n. 153, p. 268. Alberto Sartoris wrote on this subject: "When he was called up as an Artillery officer, he left Como quietly for the war to do his duty as an Italian soldier. He left unobtrusively, with natural simplicity, exemplary dignity, without ostentation and without engaging in any useless trivialities". Alberto Sartoris, *Presenza di Giuseppe Terragni. Prima mostra commemorativa di Giuseppe Terragni,* exhibition catalogue (Como, Salone del Broletto, July 27-August 10, 1949).

11. On December 4th, 1940, Alberto Sartoris wrote to Terragni from Rome to tell him he had spoken with Oppo who had commented that Terragni was on the list for an important commission for the E42 Universal Exposition, without specifying any details. Martina Sommella Grossi in *Giuseppe Terragni. Opera completa,* op. cit., p. 581.

12. Letter from Terragni to Cereghini, June 1st, 1939, cited in Paolo Nicolosio, *Lingeri e Terragni* in *Pietro Lingeri,* op. cit., p. 65.

2

3

The procedure for consent for this housing was complicated. The Municipal Council was undecided on the number of apartments to be built, and considerable time passed before they reached the decision, by which time Terragni had already left for the army. The new version foresaw the elimination of one of the three buildings, and building permits were granted only in January 1942, when Terragni was already in Russia.[13] The housing was completed in May 1943 when Terragni had returned from Russia a few months earlier, and the outcome of the war was far different from what had been envisaged when he had left. There is no information about any particular interest shown by Terragni concerning this quite modest project on his return to Como. Far more enticing was another commission that was advanced in June 1939 by Umberto Bernasconi, director of the magazine, *Origini* and fiduciary of the local Portuense-Monteverde Fascist Group. This concerned the realisation of a new Casa del Fascio in Rome, and although nothing had been officially confirmed, it seemed to be a solid proposal.[14] A short time later, a layout plan of the area was sent to his studio: seemingly a good sign. The problem was that no detailed plans had yet been drawn up for the area, so there was no information concerning the boundaries of the site and the relative urban planning regulations. Despite this fact, obsessed with the idea of building in Rome, Terragni immersed himself in the work, drawing up layout plans that he took to Rome to understand the actual intentions of the commissioning body. His initial plan was to extend the building to the other side of the road to divide the structure into two buildings united by means of an overhead pedestrian bridge. That was not all; he also planned to create a square in front of both sites to form an authentic proscenium or fore-stage on the banks of the Tiber, over which it would be possible to create a new river crossing. In this way, Rome, like Como, would possess a Casa del Fascio that would become part of a monumental urban plan, or rather, monumental and abstract at the same time. But Terragni's determination did not coincide with the apathy in Rome. Once again, he returned to Como empty-handed and the situation was left aside for at least a year.

In September 1940, the commissioning body contacted Terragni again. Italy had been at war for two months and Lieutenant Terragni had been moved from Cremona to Schio. Once again, without an official

13. For details on the data and timeframe concerning the housing project in via Anzani, refer to the data sheet by Maria Sommella Grossi published in *Giuseppe Terragni. Opera completa.* op. cit., pp. 578-581.

14. For details on the data and timeframe concerning the Casa del Fascio in Rome, refer to the data sheet by Giorgio Ciucci published in *Giuseppe Terragni. Opera completa.* op. cit., pp. 594-602.

commission, and in the middle of his army drill, Terragni developed his project further, and when he was on leave in Como, he drew up the working plans necessary for initial authorisations. This was at the project phase that today would be considered the final stage, but in the meantime, another problem appeared. The proposed building would be erected on a site that, in the new detailed plan that had just been approved, was destined for a multi-lane arterial road that would connect the district of Monteverde with the E42 site. This deadlock, plus the war, led to the umpteenth collapse of any project in Rome. From the Rationalist-Abstract viewpoint, the Portuense-Monteverde Casa del Fascio design could be considered as a criticism of the project, over-embellished with arches and columns, that the Piacentini group was constructing at the EUR, only a few kilometres away. Terragni replied with two clean buildings connected by an overhead pedestrian bridge which, in a moment when the prophecy of Modernism was being contaminated, seemed to pay homage to that architecture 'designed by engineers' to which, as a staunch Rationalist, Terragni felt it was essential to return.

As mentioned above, the project foresaw two buildings erected on two distinct plots: the first, or main building, was to house the Casa del Fascio itself, while the other, the assembly hall. With the design of the Casa del Fascio in particular, it is clear that the aim was to create a classical monumental composition, not obtained through "citing" other styles, but using modern analytical methods. This was a concept expressed by Terragni himself with regard to the project for the Palazzo dei ricevimenti e congressi, when he reaffirmed the "spiritual" need for a layout based on the Golden Ratio. However, if the Classical style of the Palazzo dei ricevimenti e congressi was proposed as a "citation", albeit in a stylised manner, the Roman Casa del Fascio was designed using a deliberately abstract language composed only of pillars and horizontal and vertical planes linked with one another. It was a means of expression that, at the time, typified the abstractionism of the Como painters of the 1930s like Radice, Rho, and Carla Badiali, to whom Terragni made explicit reference. For all these artists, abstract composition was based on a few fundamental geometrical figures, balanced shapes and colours through empirical cross-references and relationships in a manner to determine, in its entirety, an equilibrium and restraint that, by analogy, evoked classicism.[15]

15. In reference to the relationship between lyrical rationalist painting and Terragni's architecture, Fabio Mariano wrote: "the refined bi-dimensional deconstruction, the sliding of geometrical figures superimposed in successive layers, each one leaving the mark of layers of different colour washes, without ever seeking to create depth, but being satisfied with the Mondrian-style balance achieved through the composition of visual weight, corresponds directly with a comparable possibility of architectural modulation of the plane, section and plan. Fabio Mariano, *Poesia della razionalità*, Istituto Mides, Rome, 1983, p. 11. *Giuseppe Terragni. Poesia della razionalità*, exhibition catalogue edited by Fabio Mariano and Luigi Ferrario. To understand the classical aspirations of Terragni's poetic, and more generally, the whole concept of Como Abstractionism, it is worth reading the excellent book by Gino Severini *Du cubisme au classicisme*, J. Povololozky Editeurs, Paris, 1921. A fundamental text for an understanding of lyrical Rationalism is the publication by Nathalie Vernizzi, *Razionalismo lirico. Ricerca sulla pittura astratta in Italia*, All'insegna del pesce d'oro, Milan, 1994. Also recommended: Luciano Caramel, *L'eredità di Terragni e l'architettura italiana 1943-1968*, Convention proceedings, Como, 14-15 September, 1968, in *L'Architettura. Cronache e Storia*, n. 163, p. 12. Of historical interest are testimonies by two of those who lived during that period: Alberto Sartoris, *La lunga marcia dell'arte astratta in Italia*, Vanni Scheiwiller editore, Milan, 1980; Pietro Maria Bardi, *Il volto del secolo. La prima cellula dell'architettura razionalista in Italia*, Pier Luigi Librino editore, Bergamo, 1988.

Consequently – new expressive modalities would express an ancient intent, or even more, an intent that was classically ageless and suspended in time. In fact, Terragni and his abstractionist friends saw in ancient paintings, especially those of the early Renaissance, like the works of Masaccio, Beato Angelico, and Piero della Francesca, the codes of this harmony that paradoxically could be exported into Modernism, especially in architecture. This theory, proposed by another outstanding figure from Como, the intellectual and art critic Massimo Bontempelli, was their utopia: probably naive, certainly evocative; incomprehensible outside the infernal, fertile and contradictory Italian culture of the 1930s.[16] A comment by the painter, Mario Radice, Terragni's close friend and creator of the abstract panels in the Casa del Fascio in Como, sums it all up: "No work of art exists without rhythm (for us, painters, sculptors and architects) it is the way of life of ordered space – therefore, without formal order there is no art, order is the infinite harmony of the different parts; in turn, harmony is the according of elements, and therefore their unification. According (from cor, cordis) means filling a gap or interval, and placing the elements of the composition in relation with one another"[17]; therefore – according the elementary and the empiric, obtained through plastic harmonisation and the juxtaposition of elements, and also through their chromatic balance. With the front facade of the Casa del Fascio, Terragni balanced the horizontality of the projecting balconies with the verticality of the heraldic frame on the other side of the facade. An abstract and anti-plastic object, which he had already used in the project for the Milan Trade Fair. At ground level, he also balanced the verticality of the carved stone wall with the horizontal line of the ramp that, after accosting the wall, was transformed to create the delicate plinth base that followed the sides of building and gave the project some of its classical quality. While Terragni applied abstract balance to the design of the Casa del Fascio, on the other side of the road, for the assembly hall he changed strategy, opting for a form that was as monolithic as possible, almost a metaphysical object. A mute volume, characterised only by the slightly curved facade: an external reflection of the orator's podium inside. In the corner, the building was peeled open to become a curved slab wall like the poetic sculptures created by Fausto Melotti at that time. The analytical form was woven together with the form a priori, the open blended with the closed,

16. It is worth reading Massimo Bontempelli, *L'avventura novecentista*, Vallecchi edizioni, Florence, 1938 and *Realismo magico e altri scritti sull'arte*, Abscondita edizioni, Milan, 2006. Concerning the relationship between Terragni and Bontempelli see: "Francesco Tentori, Terragni e Bontempelli: architettura e letteratura" in *Giuseppe Terragni. Opera completa*, op. cit., pp. 207-215.

17. Mario Radice in *Chiarimenti*, reproduced by Guido Ballo, Mario Radice, ILTE, Turin, 1973, p. 184. Cited by Nathalie Vernizzi, *Razionalismo lirico. Ricerca sulla pittura astratta in Italia*, op. cit., p. 257.

4

obtained through the balancing of different components, resulting in an Abstractionism which is more evoked than represented: ultimately, abstract Classicism. This is the nature of the Roman Casa del Fascio: a project that seems to summarise the research that Terragni had continued throughout the 1930s and in this way, it closed an era.

However, at the time of his departure, the most urgent, and surely the most concrete assignment for the studio was the Giuliani-Frigerio building, an apartment block intended for producing income through long term leases. Therefore, a building that needed to be constructed quickly, and more to the point, that should not be expensive.[18] Through the Novocomum company, that had commissioned their building thirteen years earlier, and that became known as the first Rationalist building in Italy, Terragni acted as intermediary to purchase a small plot of only 450 square metres not far from his first construction. The time schedule imposed by the client was very limited, so the land was purchased in January 1939, and at the end of March of the same year, the project (drawn up very rapidly) was submitted to the Municipal Council. The following month it was approved by the council and by the client who demanded the building be completed by September.[19] Those who know anything about construction are well aware that casting a reinforced concrete building on site in six months is practically impossible, but Terragni was certainly not lacking in audacity, sometimes close to bravado, and he accepted. Because of the hasty schedule, before the work started, the owner had drawn up lease contracts and relative penalties. Terragni shared this audacity and bravado with the client, Mrs Giuliani-Frigerio, an attractive woman from Milan, emancipated and determined, who could also be quite disdainful. She would arrive in Como in her showy car and issue precise instructions before returning to Milan to look after her business affairs and her superficial sophisticated social life. Her social acquaintances did not disdain "modern" interior design, especially in bathrooms and kitchens, with refreshing new elegance like the designs of Gio Ponti. It was probably the socialite class's infatuation for the new style that pushed Mrs Giuliani-Frigerio to grant the commission to someone who was considered the most "modern" architect of the moment. However, this choice did not consider the fact that for Terragni, Modernism was not a question of fashion, but a mission, in fact, a prophecy.

18. For details concerning the data and timeframe of the Giuliani-Frigerio building, refer to the data sheets by Elisabetta Terragni (from where the quotes were taken) published in *Giuseppe Terragni. Opera completa.* op. cit., pp. 584-594. Also see Luca Lanini, *Commento in Quindici anni di vita e lavoro con l'amico e maestro architetto Giuseppe Terragni,* op. cit., pp. 131-135.

19. Initially the client had requested a courtyard building, but given the limited size of the plot, Terragni, convinced her to change her mind.

5

Inevitably, there was conflict between them; between the radical and far from accommodating architect, and the determined woman, used to getting what she wanted in life, and rapidly. The conflict was recorded in the documents that were sent through Terragni's trusted assistant, Luigi Zuccoli, left alone to deal with the commissions[20] after the two brothers, Attilio and Giuseppe, were called up for the army. To understand the tone of the relations between the client and the architect, there is a quote from one of the many letters, dated September 20th, 1939, which was ten days before the scheduled work completion: "I require, with maximum urgency, the plans/drawings of the doors and windows of the Federation offices facing via Malta […] because, as you know, they are already leased. I wish you to know that I most certainly do not want that band of glass brick which I find hideous. Furthermore, there is positively no reason to throw money away, especially since these are only for office use […] please try to obtain a permit because it is absolutely necessary for a decision concerning the 'framing cages' around the building and the shutters".

In this letter, Mrs Guliani Frigerio was referring to the elegant framework attached to one of the facades on the west side, where the architect had planned to install folding panels or shade awnings, but that were never installed. Today, the framework appears aerial, simple, and wonderfully aesthetic. In spite of this, for the most part, the building is faithful to the project design. An impossible time schedule and a difficult client for a complex and carefully structured building with unusual features, especially for "rented housing". A project that was so rich and diverse, above all in the finishes, that Terragni was forced to control the work through the large model on a 1:50 scale, of which only a few photos remain. An extremely detailed model which seems surprising today, because this design shows how, with some of his ideas for the Giuliani-Frigerio building, Terragni foresaw the style of the post-war apartment buildings built later in cheapened and stereotyped versions. It was inevitable that when the client realised the planned schedule was improbable, she increased her visits to Como, often arriving unannounced in the studio or on site, forcing Zuccoli to cut costs and make changes, especially with regard to the size of the apartments to adapt them to the needs of the tenants. Zuccoli wrote to Lieutenant Terragni who was now away from the studio: "The client continues

20. There were four Terragni brothers: Attilio, the oldest who had fought in the Fitst World War with his father, and who was an engineer and became the Podestà of Como; Alberto dealt with the financial part of the studio, and married Signora Reginella to whom Terragni dedicated a touching portrait. She welcomed Giuseppe into her home in Olgiate Comasco during his convalescence following the Russian Campaign. Between Attilio and Alberto, was Silvio, who died young in a car accident, and finally, the youngest, Giuseppe. Engineer Attilio was also called up in the Second World War after his brother Giuseppe, and as an officer, was sent to Rhodes, where, immediately after his return to Italy, his garrison was executed by the Germans after the armistice of September 8th, 1943.

to change the size of the apartments [...]. She is convinced you have no interest at all in her building". This was not true, the extensive correspondence between the two shows this was quite the contrary. For example, Terragni wrote to Zuccoli in mid-November, 1939: "I have no news about the work. Is it possible that everything is proceeding so well that there is no need for my intervention? Could you try and send more information [...] I don't know if I will be able to continue my inspections on Sundays because things are changing here in Verona". In fact, in November, Terragni was transferred from Cremona to Verona, which made travel to Como increasingly more difficult.

As was predictable, the building was not finished at the end of 1939, so, like other tenants, the National Fascist Federation of Trade Cooperatives, which was to have rented offices on the mezzanine floor, demanded withdrawal from the contract with relative damages. Inevitably, the client laid the blame on the architect, not only for the completion delay that was postponed until June 1940, but also for the disproportionate increase in costs; the final cost on completion was 75% more than the hasty initial estimate. The client was furious: "You have had fun demolishing the work I have done, and have wasted time with decisions that needed to be made urgently", and she criticised the "extremely disorganised construction management". That was not all. In the legal proceedings between the client and Terragni, she was evidently so exasperated that she reached the point of deriding the architect. Because of the compositional balance of the facade weight and measurements, Terragni had designed the windows so that the tops of the roller shutters were flush with the ceiling. For this reason he installed the roller shutter coffer at floor level. This inversion demanded an opening and closing system controlled by "external and internal pulleys, counter-weights and roller wheels", obviously contested by the client, who promised: "I will personally pay to have photographs taken and I will have them published in *Domus* as a brilliant example of modern architecture". As can be seen in the voluminous correspondence with Zuccoli, for the whole of 1940 and the following year when Terragni left for the Russian Front, the legal and financial procedure (the client blocked all payment during the legal action) was the main concern of the studio in considerable difficulty.

Even writing from Russia, when the building had been finished for a year, Terragni persisted with Zuccoli and probably with his brother Attilio, asking that they work to recover the money owed, but it seems that, apart from the initial payment, the fees were never paid. Beyond the dispute with the client, the building remains the last project built by Terragni. A subject of considerable debate, very often respected by architectural critics, and sometimes, as in the case of Peter Eisenman, even highly praised.[21] It was a design that was already mentioned in the first critical surveys like those of Mario Labò, who edited the first monograph on Terragni's work in 1947. In the Giuliani-Frigerio building, he saw that "harmonious dissymmetry" that we have already described and that, in the 1970s, Eisenman considered as the emblematic expression of an architecture based on "pure expression", now liberated from the naturalist obligation of having to represent something other than itself.[22] Furthermore, the Giuliani-Frigerio building shows a Terragni who appears less abstract than in the past, more material, more willing to express himself through the grain and colour of materials, moving beyond the tone-on-tone for which he was recognised until that time. It is probable that the experience of designing apartment buildings in Milan with Lingeri made him more aware of the needs of a clientele whose tastes may have been further away from the absolute whiteness of the purists.[23]

However, it is Terragni himself, with his meaningful photomontage, who provides us with the reason for this work. The photo shows a corner building, with its cut out and recessed spaces, its open and enclosed corners in juxtaposition. Alongside this photo, is a detail of the facade of the Cathedral of Cremona, the city where Terragni spent his time in the army. This proximity proposed by Terragni is enigmatic, but the enigma disappears if it is considered from the viewpoint of what inspired Terragni's profound artistic sensitivity: analogy. In the photo of the cathedral, Terragni focused on details which seem like a list of different musical scores and their rhythms, from a blind wall to the facade, perforated by the rose window, the ogival arches over the entrance, the rhythmic effect of the densely arranged Gothic columns, and the broad Renaissance colonnade at ground level. The framing of Terragni's photo of the cathedral demonstrates the power of analogy. It shows how, when cleverly balanced, different

21. Mario Labò, *Giuseppe Terragni*, Milan, Il Balcone edizioni, 1947. Peter Eisenman, *Giuseppe Terragni: trasformazioni e scomposizioni critiche*, Quodlibet edizioni, Macerata, 2004. However the first articles written by Peter Eisenman on Terragni appeared in 1971 in the magazine, *Perspecta*.

22. Even in the 1950s, in the Giuliani-Frigerio building, Zevi saw a manneristic evolution of constructivism. (Bruno Zevi, *Storia dell'architettura moderna*, Giulio Einaudi editore, Turin, 1950, pp. 247-248). Bruno Zevi, *The Modern Language of Architecture*, Seattle, University of Washington Press, 1978. Also see Bruno Zevi, *Giuseppe Terragni*, Zanichelli, Bologna, 1980, p. 166.

23. Zevi wrote: "The Giuliani-Frigerio building seems to couple sacrifice with creative joy; pure burnt disappointment with an act of optimism and idealism. In spite of everything, Terragni continues to design, remaining faithful to his capacity to assert (his ideas). He would like to preserve himself for the future. But he won't succeed". Bruno Zevi, *L'Architettura. Cronaca e storie*, op. cit., p. 266.

6

rhythms and *metrons* can discover an unexpected harmony with each other. The same harmony can be transferred to modern buildings, in fact, Terragni's photomontage seems to represent an essay on the theory of architecture; given the stylization of the elements, it is the language of abstractionism that best expresses the analogous timeless harmony of the *metron*. In the 1930s, Massimo Bontempelli wrote that a figurative painting is a 'representation' defined in space and time, while an abstract work is a 'concept', or something that transcends time and space since it focuses on the quintessential structure of the subject.[24] Abstractionism is therefore a new form of metaphysics, like the ultimate opportunity for expression, that through analogy, places itself above all styles, creating a summary of the whole. The final works by Terragni sought to embody this aspiration, resulting in their indefinable unique poetic nature.

The other large project on the desk in Terragni's studio the day he left, was the so-called Casa Vietti in the neglected working-class quarter of Cortesella which Terragni had accepted to partially rebuild. This project became famous for the large bridge structure erected over the building: one of the first megastructures of Modernism. The history of the Casa Vietti project is complex, rooted in the local controversies, of which Terragni was an integral part ever since the Novocomum affair.[25] In 1939, the superintendent, Professor Chierici, had assigned him the project directly for the restoration of the semi-ruin and, on the same plot, the construction of a building that was still to be established. Terragni presented a project in June 1939, three months before his army call-up.
In the project, he proposed to preserve only the loggia, demolishing the rest of the old building, and constructing a light new pavilion with a modern, aerial, lattice design in sharp contrast with the underlying heavy Romanesque structure; in contrast, but also in analogy with it. And in fact, once more he applied the musical score rhythm; the *metron*, made abstract in modern design to determine a consonance, a dialogue, similar to that created between the Giuliani-Frigerio building and the Cathedral of Cremona. On the main facade, Terragni decided to fill the space between the loggia and the new building with a projecting terrace to form a grandiloquent open-air podium, thirteen metres above the piazza below. He planned the structure over the whole length of the plot to guarantee maximum

24. Massimo Bontempelli, *L'avventura novecentista*, op. cit., p. 176.

25. For details concerning data and timeframe of work on Casa Vietti refer to the data sheet by Attilio Terragni published in *Giuseppe Terragni. Opera completa*. op. cit., pp. 603-607. Also see Luca Lanini, *Commento in Quindici anni di vita e lavoro con l'amico e maestro architetto Giuseppe Terragni*, op. cit., pp. 119-121.

natural light penetration through changes of direction and recessed spaces, giving the overall project its specific sense of aerial lightness. Terragni drew up two projects for Casa Vietti. The first in 1939, and the other, two years later before he left for Russia. The second project was delayed because in the meantime a client had been found: the Association of Wounded War Veterans. The plan was on a 1:50 scale, practically a working plan. In February 1941, the plans, drawn up with the studio engineer Renato Uslenghi while Terragni was in the army, were submitted to the city council for approval. However, an episode disturbed the continuation of the process. During the stabilization and restoration work carried out by the Terragni studio, the ruins were set on fire and destroyed by felons hired by a faction that had planned some large real estate speculation in Cortesella, and who did not want to see any public interest in the new neighbourhood. The increasingly urgent situation with the war determined the outcome of the affair. On June 10th, 1941, the Como Municipal Council informed Terragni that the almost one million lire needed to build the pavilion was no longer available and consequently, the project was stopped. The outcome was predictable. After the war, in the frenzy of reconstruction, the burnt rubble of the ex-Casa Vietti was permanently cleared away.

In 1940, despite the fact he was increasingly more involved with army manoeuvres, Terragni was convinced he could still win the architectural battle, and worked even harder. He wrote a "Discorso ai Comaschi" (Speech to the people of Como) that began precisely with the thorny subject of Cortesella and Casa Vietti.[26] He explained to the public the difference between one faction composed of the Municipal Council, the Superintendence, and Terragni himself, and the other consisting of those heavily involved in speculation who do not accept interventions that are very far from their objectives. The article was written in stiff grandiose prose, with a rhetorical style that did not suit Terragni's normal blunt character; every time he addressed the ruling classes, he always seemed to have trouble finding appropriate language and behaviour. Despite this, the text clearly repeated the principle that he had drafted a few years earlier for the Plan for Como, where he sought a balance between the magnificent historic buildings and modern necessity, a theory that had been expressed also by Mussolini.

26. Quote from Enrico Mantero, *Giuseppe Terragni e la città del razionalismo italiano*, Dedalo edizioni, Rome, 1983, pp. 45-52.

At that time Leo Longanesi had written rather caustically "The Duce is always right". In his article, Terragni continued, saying it was therefore essential not to follow the speculators, but the guarantors of Fascist orthodoxy, in other words, the public authorities and the architect. The article pleased the powerful and protective National Minister for Education, Giuseppe Bottai, who wrote to Terragni immediately as follows: "Dear Terragni, I read your interesting speech to Como in the Ambrosiano. Your calm honest words on such a sensitive subject are worthy of praise. I thank you and send cordial best wishes, Yours, Bottai".[27] Two years later, when Terragni was on the verge of another winter on the Russian Front, Bottai elected him as part of the fifth section of the National Board of Education, Sciences and Arts.[28] Being in the good graces of such a powerful man was no small privilege, but just as he had done with Margherita Sarfatti, Mussolini's long-time mistress and godmother of the Italian Novecento movement, Terragni was never capable of taking advantage of these friendships: an inability that would cost him dearly in the disastrous events of the war. On receiving Bottai's telegram, after advance notice from his conciliatory older brother, Attilio, Terragni insisted on the need for controversy, convinced that it was time to wage a battle against the bourgeois with their "small-town mentality" who fought their speculation battles in the local newspapers.

He incited his brother to contact Superintendent Chierici who had assigned him the project, to find a common course of action to continue the battle. Meanwhile, he decided to contact the new Podestà of Como who had replaced his brother, and wrote a short note, congratulating him on his nomination with the hope that "your appointment to this important and sensitive office will coincide with the conclusion of those conflicts that we have fought together several times, and that this will mark the beginning of a golden age for Fascism in Como. Till we meet again at the Casa del Fascio in Como. Yours, Terragni".[29] This was his last official move to save the Casa Vietti project.

A move that shows a Terragni in 1940, more energetic than ever, and not at all worried about a future focussed on ambitious retribution. As well, life in the army, which he rarely mentioned in his letters to Zuccoli, did not seem to bother him at all. He had always had deep admiration for military life and anything connected with uniforms, weapons and life in the barracks.

27. Ivi, p. 49.

28. Telegram from Bottai to Terragni dated April 2nd, 1942: "I am happy to inform you that with the provision currently under signature, you have been called to be part of the fifth section of the National Board of Education, Sciences and Arts. National Ministry for Education, Bottai". (Source, Terragni Archives).

29. Source, Terragni Archives, cited in the Attilio Terragni profile published in *Giuseppe Terragni. Opera completa*. op. cit., pp. 603-607.

7

8

This fervour was felt by all the family. Giuseppe's dour father, Michele, had based his life on military principles and discipline, applying them successfully in his professional life. Michele, and Giuseppe's oldest brother, Attilio, had both fought in the First World War, and still today in the family home, there is an album with photos of the Great War, taken by Attilio. The subjects are mainly glimpses of military life, with companions and fellow soldiers shown during daily life in the trenches, but photographed to avoid showing the misery and frustration of a life narrated by others in a far less heroic manner. These glimpses came to life again, but in another tonality, in the photos taken by Giuseppe in Yugoslavia and in Russia. To understand how much Terragni was attracted to military life, one needs only remember one of his large-scale portraits, painted the year after his military service in 1929, when he was 25. It shows a self-portrait in uniform. The painting, blatantly executed in the style of Sironi, shows Terragni in the foreground, with his face turned slightly towards the viewer, as if bolstered by his blue platoon cape of which, according to Zuccoli, he was very proud.[30] Behind him are three artillerymen focused on loading a canon. The style is the Italian Novecento school he always adopted when painting: monumental and statuesque, where wide bands of brown contain splashes of more vibrant colour. The shadows are more obvious than necessary to provide a plastic three dimensional effect. The painting, like the fine preparatory sketches, clearly reveal his undeniable satisfaction in seeing himself dressed this way, as if this uniform (from the First World War) was the most appropriate for his personality. We find this attraction for military uniforms again, more than ten years after the self-portrait with the blue cape. An attraction of a completely different kind. In 1943, when he returned following the defeat in Russia, deeply disturbed and in a fragile mental condition, he would wander around Como with his threadbare army coat that he refused to remove, even though it was late spring in Como. For Terragni, his coat was symbolic of the survivor who had been forced to return home. Its role, so different from the self-portrait in uniform, was worn to demonstrate to the world that he had not betrayed his country, that he was not a deserter. Worn in plain view through the streets of Como, by a heavy-set man, 6 foot 2 inches tall, his coat did not pass unnoticed. Had anyone wanted to look for Terragni the deserter, they only had to stop him in the street.

30. "In 1928, Terragni was serving as an artillary officer and was proud of his uniform and above all, the blue cape that he wrapped around himself with satisfaction, attracting considerable feminine attention", Luigi Zuccoli, *Quindici anni di vita e di lavoro con l'amico e maestro architetto Giuseppe Terragni*, op. cit., p. 59. On this subject, there is a useful observation by Paolo Fossati: "The self-portrait in officer's uniform shows the painter in a role as an authoritative leader of men. Patriotic, but not heroic (engaged in his own fashion); so this is the other side of the apprentice we know, his role as a young artist seen as a leader of men and as a functional figure involved in social service. So, the portrait that Terragni shows during official visits should be read as a moralized self-portrait: otherwise, how can we define the painted figure that shows the artist as a responsible and capable leader of men", Paolo Fossati, *Il pittore: ufficiale e gentiluomo* in *Giuseppe Terragni. Opera completa*, op. cit., p. 108.

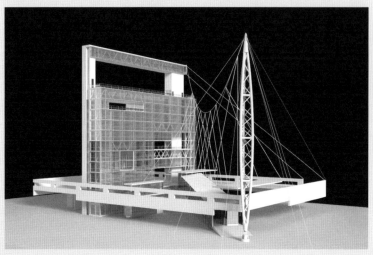

9

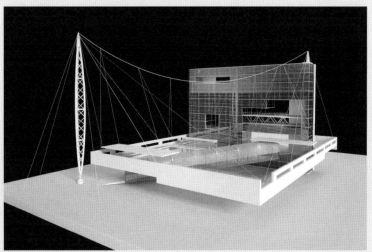

10

This was the ultimate bravado from a man who always carried the weight of his personal choices on his shoulders, who could not conceive recanting his personal convictions, who refused to conform with the small-minded, middle class perspective of those always careful to defend their privileges and commonplace lives. His coat bore witness to a road that began with the impeccable blue cloak in his self-portrait and ended with the threadbare coat worn during his final days through the streets of Como. In July, 1943, when Terragni died on the stairs of his fiancé's house, despite the fact it was mid-summer, he was inevitably wearing his coat. In the pockets were dried flowers, picked in the Russian steppe.[31]

Terragni spent the end of 1939 and the following year in Cremona, Verona and Schio, from where he sent his plans for the Roman Casa del Fascio, to Como. He was fully occupied with army life but did not neglect his work for the studio. 1940 was a year of intense work. Despite being in the army, it was one of the most productive years in his short career. As well as the Roman Casa del Fascio, in autumn 1939, he worked with Pietro Lingeri on a preliminary plan for the headquarters of the Fascist Institute of Glass and Ceramics to be built in Milan. It was a dull functional project where the two adjacent buildings, joined by stairways and services, can be clearly identified as the work of Lingeri alone.[32] However, the project in Milan opened the door to another project of far greater size and prominence, and this time Terragni committed himself personally without intermediaries. This was between the summer and autumn of 1939. Pier Maria Bardi and Ortensio Gatti worked to obtain a prestigious assignment for Terragni and Pier Luigi Nervi, increasingly more present: the Pavilion for the Italian Glass Makers Union at the E42 Universal Exposition. This was proof that Piacentini's academic front line was no longer as unassailable as it had been a few years earlier; it was the moment to "set up a studio in Rome". For Terragni, this project should have represented the official entrance of Abstract Rationalism in Rome, as can be seen in the letter he wrote to Pier Maria Bardi, protector of Italian Rationalism in Rome, on July 18th, 1939, (two months before his departure): "Dear Bardi, thank you for your kind mark of friendship […] Today I hope to meet Gatti who for some time has been making vague comments about the possibility of the Glass Pavilion for the E42. Galvanise Neri for the good cause. We will win this infinite battle of Modern

31. On this subject, Alberto Sartoris wrote: "Although he was fighting in the endless Russian steppe, he wrote regularly to his dearest friends, sending news of his observations. He remained focused on his art, and although he was part of an enormous tragic drama, it did not undermine his curiosity and imagination. While fighting a war in often horrific conditions, this mystic blend of action and energy, still managed to give shape and clarity to his theories, his architecture, and his science. He even found the time and opportunity to make sketches and send them from the banks of the Don to his faithful companions left at home. Alberto Sartoris, *Presenza di Giuseppe Terragni* in *Prima mostra commemorativa di Giuseppe Terragni*, exhibition catalogue, op. cit.

32. Antonio Brucculeri, *Progetto di massima per l'Istituto fascista del vetro e della ceramica* in *Pietro Lingeri*, edited by Chiara Baglione and Elisabetta Susani, op. cit., p. 290.

architecture if we plant our elbows into the ribs of those lazy people and Camorrist mobsters in the E42 bunch. We of the old architectural guard will build an island of iron and glass and… fire in the dangerous slimy sea in the Three Fountains district".[33] In another letter to Bardi two years later, on November 30th, 1941, from the Russian Front, he continued to reiterate on the subject: "Dear Bardi, […] I am preparing a huge amount of documentary photographic material […]. When it is a done deal and victory has been achieved, we will use it to take out the terrible Ojetti and his Ojettini (followers). We will have some fun and this time we will create the museum of horrors in the rooms of the Glass Building at the Universal Exposition".[34] Very few sketches, fairly congruent with each other, remain for the Union Pavilion. There are three drafts of fascinating reconstructions, three plausible variations on the theme.[35] In all three there is a large rectangular enclosure in golden section containing a long ramp that crosses it to reach the first level of a fine lamella that transversally slices through the enclosure. Rather than a building, the lamella rises like an advertising hoarding demonstrating the potential available with huge sheets of glass, recently put into production. In two of the three projects, on the external corner of the enclosure, is a tall steel lattice pylon (more probably made of aluminium, given the autarchy) that simultaneously suspends the large enclosure and the ramp that crosses it. In one version there is a single pylon and the cables on the other side are attached to the top level of the lamella; in the other, there are two pylons positioned on the opposite shorter sides of the enclosure. There is no doubt that the most exciting solutions are those with the pylons and cables which seem to split the air indicating the directional lines of force of the composition.[36]

Observing the project, one has the impression that Terragni wanted to send a response to Le Corbusier and his Palace of the Soviets: both structures feature paratactic compositions of single elements separated in relation to one another; while Le Corbusier's structure seems to define a monumentalization of functionalism, Terragni's version bears no trace of functionalism. According to Manfredo Tafuri, in the 1930s Terragni had "launched a challenge on transparency of language".[37] A mannerist challenge in which functionalism, which was one of the foundations of the Modern Movement, had transcended into a dimension

33. Ada F. Marcianò, *Giuseppe Terragni, Opera completa 1925-1943*, edited by Giorgio Ciucci, Officina edizioni, Rome, p. 330.

34. Quote from id., *Giuseppe Terragni, Opera completa 1925-1943*, op. cit., p. 330.

35. The reconstructions are taken from the book by Flavio Mangione, Luca Ribichini and Attilio Terragni, *Giuseppe Terragni a Roma*, Prospettive, Rome, 2015.

36. Valerio Paolo Mosco, "Un progetto attualissimo" in *Perché l'architettura italiana ora e altri scritti*, Edizioni Are, Rome, 2017, pp. 33-46.

37. Manfredo Tafuri, "Il soggetto e la maschera. Un'introduzione a Giuseppe Terragni", in *Lotus International*, n. 20, September, 1978.

that was now completely satisfied with itself, its rhythmic balances, and its abstract analogies. Tafuri wrote: "For Terragni, outside that analytical work, there is nothing else: no 'argument', no message, no 'noise'". Tafuri felt that all that remained was the stage setting, or rather, the abstract stage setting. On this subject he spoke about "masks" and these could appear to be the composing elements of the Italian Glass Makers Union project. The large enclosure, the pylons, the glass lamella can be compared to masks: Pirandellian masks, symbolically held together by the cables that split the air. Masks that seem to stage a metaphysical, emphatic, suspended script, in which the architectural, paradisal, and enigmatic, although modern, characters are clothed in costumes of the myth with which they intend to celebrate their magical apparition. Tafuri went even further, and through his Pirandellian interpretation, sketched the portrait of the author of the work: "Terragni is already, in himself, a Pirandellian character. For him, reality and appearance are equivalent existential dimensions: the ultimate game will be when one penetrates the other until the mask becomes reality and within it, dissolves every volition of form". Perhaps an appealing interpretation, but misleading. The masks that Tafuri saw were not accurate. The objects that Terrragni placed on his stage set (pylon, cables, enclosure, glass lamella, ramp) did have a face, albeit an abstract face, no longer naturalistic or materialistic. They were objects elevated in an atmosphere half-way between the inescapable and the transcendent: they were the hypostasis of Modernism, of its quintessential stylizations. Comparing the characters in this project as such, had nothing to do with Pirandello's theatrical nihilism, and even less with the middle-class boredom of the young *indifferent* characters described by Moravia, also evoked by Tafuri. On the contrary, Terragni's characters referred to another Modernism, that of T. S. Eliot, Paul Klee, and Benjamin Britten, a Modernism that retained its spirituality, and within it, found its lyrical nature.

In the same fertile year, 1940, Terragni drafted another project for the E42, this time a pavilion for the Railway Exposition. A project that anticipated the large steel and glass showcases that Mies van der Rohe was to create in the United States after the war. This project was followed by others, drafted with sketches, for a cinema-theatre,

11

12

a summer camp, an exposition pavilion in Lissone, a partially covered stadium, and a standardised petrol station whose image was based on roofing composed of lenticular steel elements set on lenticular pillars. The petrol station is an image that reaffirms the potential of lyrical Abstractionism in a more technical dimension. So, in the army, he drafted projects in the barracks, and now and then went to Como to see how things were progressing at the studio.

He continued with this lifestyle while the war seemed destined for a crushing victory by the German troops who were applying their Blitzkrieg tactics- the rapid unpredicted penetration of armoured tanks far into the enemy lines. Within a few months they had conquered Czechoslovakia, Belgium, Holland, Denmark, Norway and the parts of Finland and Poland assigned to Germany in the 1939 agreements between the Reich and the Soviet Union.

In the spring of 1940, the Wehrmacht attacked France, swerving around the Maginot Line, and putting to flight what had been considered until then the most efficient army in Europe. It was an unprecedented defeat for France. Paris fell in June 1940, and a few days later, accompanied by his architect, Albert Speer, Hitler strolled around a deserted Paris at dawn, discussing plans for building a (new) Berlin that would surpass the monumental splendour of the French capital.

Meanwhile, the French Army fled northwards with the English troops to the port of Dunkirk. In an audacious, heroic and fortuitous episode, a large part of the troops was saved by hundreds of English leisure boats; this was happening while in London, Parliament was divided, trying to decide between continuing a war that seemed in a disastrous state, or signing a treaty with the German dictator. On August 10th, 1940, in a bombastic announcement by the Duce to an excited injudicious crowd, Italy declared war on France and England. Mussolini went to war with an army that was ill-prepared but convinced of an imminent victory. He entered the conflict with a very precise plan: to convince Germany to concede Italian supremacy over North Africa, the Balkans, and Greece, where Italy already controlled the Dodecanese. The euphoria in the final months of 1940 spread through the troops, and the fact that, in attacking a France in its death throes, the Royal Italian Army only managed to conquer Menton, did not seem to be of great importance.

13

The general feeling was that it was a war that was won in advance: but it was a war won by others. In this situation, Lieutenant Terragni tried to obtain, not just leave, but unlimited furlough that would have allowed him to return to Como permanently. As well, Terragni and his brother had both been in the army for years and were certainly not unknown in the Fascist chain of command: suffice to say that until a short time before, Attilio had been the Podestà of Como. Already before Italy entered the war, in May 1940, Terragni's friend Valdimeri had tried to intervene in his favour. Valdimeri was the Director of the Brera Academy who had commissioned the building for the new academy and for the Danteum.

Valdimeri had written to the authorities stating that "Terragni's work is fundamental for completing the Danteum".[38] Perhaps the request was sent too late, but the manoeuvres for obtaining his furlough fell through right at that time. In May, evidently instructed by someone in authority, or by Valdameri himself, a director at the Ministry of War sent a telegram to the high command where Terragni was stationed, to request exceptional unlimited leave. The Commander of the Armed Forces, Sorice, examined the question and wrote to Minister Bottai who had probably intervened on the question of Terragni's leave. Sorice wrote: "Your Excellency, I have taken a close interest in your request concerning Complement Lieutenant Giuseppe Terragni, but unfortunately, given the current situation, it will not be easy to satisfy this officer. However, I will inform you if there is any further news. Please accept, Your Excellency, the expression of my respectful esteem".[39] The news that followed was not good. This time, Lieutenant Colonel Zuppani, commander of the consigned troops, stated that the 33rd Mobile Survey Division, of which Terragni was part, was on stand-by, and therefore "granting exceptional unlimited leave to Lieutenant Giuseppe Terragni would be possible only if he can be replaced by another equivalent officer". The letter was dated May 20th, 1940, 20 days after Italy had entered the war. However Terragni did not lose hope and in September, wrote: "They said something about unlimited leave here at the headquarters as well. We will wait and see!"[40] Zuccoli described that in the months before war was declared, Terragni could not decide whether to take advantage of this help from political acquaintances and influential figures, as his brother and family had probably

38. Letter from Valdameri on May 15th, 1940 quoted in T. L. Schumacher, *The Danteum*, Princeton Architectural Press, 1996, p. 160.

39. Giorgio Ciucci, "Terragni e l'architettura" in *Giuseppe Terragni. Opera completa*, op. cit., pp. 68-71.

40. Letter to Zuccoli on September 25th, 1949 (AGT 920).

advised him, or whether to remain in the army[41]. Once the war began, he decided on the latter; in any case, with his rash advance guard optimism, he was convinced he would be able to manage his studio, design projects even during a war, return victorious at the end of the war and "set up his studio in Rome" to construct completely modern architecture.

Between the end of 1940 and the early months of 1941 Terragni continued to travel back and forth between Cremona and Verona. He was far more militarily involved than he had been previously and his professional visits to Como became increasingly less frequent. After spending the New Year in Verona, at the end of January he was invited to the Officers' Club firing range in Nettunia, the town founded by Mussolini by combining Anzio with Nettuno. He stayed there a month. He often wrote to his collaborator, Zuccoli, and fled to Rome to see his friend Bardi so they could weave a net able to ensnare Piacentini and his group, and "enter with authority in the great Roman field of action".[42] The letters sent to Como to his collaborator Zuccoli were always focused on the same topic: the unfinished business concerning his projects, mainly about demanding outstanding payment, and the ongoing connected legal procedures. He never wrote about his army life, at least not with his subordinate. He probably wrote about the army to his fiancée or his brother, but if these letters existed, they have been lost. Another possibility, which is probable given his character, is that he considered that military matters were not a subject for civilian life: a different life. Other priorities, other schedules and other chains of command would have convinced Terragni not to overlap his two lives. Meanwhile, the war was progressing and the front lines were being defined, and with them, the role of the Italian Royal Army. In April, 1941, a year and a half after his call-up, Terragni, who was part of the Mobile Artillery Surveyor Corps, left with his battalion for Yugoslavia. He stayed there a month on the sidelines, far from the front lines. During the journey from Cremona to Venice, before the crossing to Split, he took a large number of photos. Scenes snapped from the train, Venetian and Dalmatian scenery, but military life as well. He took photos of military architecture, but also modern architecture, examples of that international Modernist style that his friend Sartoris had been collecting in his travels all over Europe. He also took photos of Roman and Byzantine ruins, seizing the

41. Luigi Zuccoli, *Quindici anni di vita e di lavoro con l'amico e maestro architetto Giuseppe Terragni*, op. cit., p. 59.

42. "...and I am sure that Cappelletti will drop the mediocre unrewarding work in Como to enter, without risk and with authority, the great Roman field of action". Letter to Zuccoli from the Albergo Minerva in Rome on February 23rd, 1941 (AGT 926). From that period, also see: letter to Zuccoli on February 18th, 1941, from Nettunia (AGT 924) and another on February 21st, 1941, also from Nettunia (AGT 925).

sculptural quality of individual ruins in their pure, timeless, monumental substance.

His other photos were focused on military life. They were mainly pictures of fellow soldiers in comradely, mocking poses that recall Terragni's spirit when he began his artistic career as a caricaturist, not long after his adolescence. These photos were little more than quick snaps that show how army life during that first year was experienced without the 'true war'. The pictures taken of landscapes and architecture during train travel have a very different tone and merit: accidental perspectives, never front-on, almost fleeting shots. For example, there is a photo taken from the train, that shows a hill with light fortifications, ramshackle palisades that mark the line of the contour. An image that is wonderfully contemporary. Modern in its framing (Terragni was an excellent painter), modern in the atmosphere that magically combines realism, constructivism, and especially, metaphysics. But Terragni's was a new form of metaphysics that had nothing in common with the rhetorical paintings of de Chirico or Carrà: a metaphysical concept that was elusive, ineffable, that seems to be telling us that the enigma is not a rebus, but the same reality seen through other eyes. Just as enigmatic and moving are the photos taken from the train of local populations in barren, rugged landscapes, amazed at the appearance of a convoy carrying soldiers from other countries to unknown destinations for unknown reasons. One of these photos, snapped quickly from the train, probably during the lengthy voyage to Russia, shows a long line of refugees fleeing from their villages with their household goods: the framing is on an angle, dynamic, Futuristic, but the subject (poor people forced to flee because of horrors caused by others) is pure Dostoevsky, steeped in a *pietas* that has nothing in common with the swaggering bravado of the advance guard. Terragni compares two contradictory worlds, but does not perceive them as contradictory: herein lies his unique nature, the deepest aspect of his personality, in both his private and artistic life. In Yugoslavia, his character seems noble, proud of that military role that allowed him to escape Como that he had found oppressive for some time, angrily describing the "stupid provincial atmosphere" that pervaded it.[43] He wrote to Zuccoli: "This town, (Split, ed.) where life is very strange, is like a Von Stroheim film. (Do you remember those great films about World War 1?)

43. Letter to Zuccoli on April 10th, 1941 (AGT 930).

14

15

An ideal place to breathe that incredible atmosphere that we coveted so much on those grey Como Sundays between the Polonio café and a stroll under the porticos".[44]

On his return to Cremona, Terragni wrote an article against the detested Ugo Ojetti, the powerful critic, enemy of Rationalism, and responsible for an unconditional return to academic architecture. The pretext was in defence of a book that Agnoldomenico Pica had written on Italian Rationalist architecture[45]. The book had been torn to shreds by Ojetti. To support his arguments, Terragni took inspiration from Diocletian's Palace that he had just visited, and more precisely, from the huge seafront wall that encloses the vestiges of the palace inside the modern town.
The massive stone wall that Terragni photographed, with its historic carvings and pillared arches, is an amazing example of Rational architecture. If we imagine taking a slice of it and considering it as a building, what would we find? Nothing more than a clean sober example of pure Rational architecture. We would find true architecture, not the false-ancient and false-modern style of the recently constructed trash that is the Palace of Italian Civilisation in Piacentino's EUR. The article should be considered as part of a wider strategy laid out by Terragni and Bardi to "enter without risk and with authority, the great Roman field of action". And again, the manoeuvre to approach Pagano should also be seen as part of the strategy. The approach probably began with a letter from Terragni which has been lost, to which Pagano replied on August 8th, 1940: "Thank you for your kind card. I appreciate your expression of friendship. You can count on me as a friend, colleague and ally in a struggle that must never divide us. It is essential that we, of the old guard, maintain that tactical and pragmatic union that has been our most effective weapon in controversy. It is important to overcome all personalism to defend the ideas, and our modern architecture which is in danger of sinking under so much compromise. I am sure of your sincere participation in this program and please feel you can count on me as a friend. I am your (friend) without grudges or envy: I appreciate your work and as you know, this is what counts. I know you are constructing a building in Como. I would be happy to publish pictures of it in *Costruzioni-Casabella* with full honours. I would also like to illustrate two of your villas: the Terragni house at Seveso, and the other on the road to Como. I would only need the plans and your

44. Letter to Zuccoli on April 23rd, 1941 (AGT 927).

45. The draft of the article is dated May 25th, 1941, and is preserved in the Terragni archives (AGT 932). The Terragni article, entitled "L'architettura di Sant'Elia rosicchiata da Ugo Ojetti", was sent to the magazine, *Origini* which did not publish it, but evidently it was read by Terragni's friends and by Pagano. Pagano's reply seems to be a comment on this article, as if thanking the author. It was published with the title "Commenti e divagazioni sulle 'Internazionali' on page 3 of the Corriere" in Enrico Mantero, *Giuseppe Terragni e la città del razionalismo italiano*, op. cit., pp. 181-187. Luca Lanini considered the text as an answer to Pagano's article published in "Costruzioni-Casabella" n. 158, February 1941, in which Pagano bitterly noted that Italian Rationalism had been cast aside by the Piacentini Imperial style of architecture endorsed by the Regime (Luca Lanini, *Commento* in Luigi Zuccoli, *Quindici anni di vita e lavoro con l'amico e maestro architetto Giuseppe Terragni*, op. cit., p. 111).

16

permission to photograph them. The costs will be paid by the magazine. I wish you good luck. Yours, G. Pagano".[46]

The relationship between Pagano and Terragni was a complex one, indicative of the situation at the time and more generally because of controversies during those years. Pagano had been very critical of the Casa del Fascio in Como. He had found the composition pretentious and felt it did not suit a form of Modernism that he interpreted in another manner, focused on social needs, therefore plain and straightforward, almost deliberately anti-poetic. Pagano was also a Fascist, but far more cognizant than Terragni, who, as Zuccoli described, had taken the Party Card with a certain offhandedness. Within complicated Fascist politics, Pagano had always supported what was defined as 'Left-wing Fascism', also known as 'Fascist mysticism'.[47] Therefore he considered Fascism as a popular movement, born with the objective of emancipating the deprived classes, but contrary to Bolshevism, the end would be achieved magically without slipping into materialism and without resorting to enforced collectivization. His beliefs were steeped in the spirit of the "squadrista" and (grass roots) movement that he had pursued since the time of his participation in the Italian Regency of Carnaro, therefore before the advent of Fascism. In the light of what we could consider his idealogical precondition, Pagano considered the Como Casa del Fascio an expression of an elitist departure from the true Fascist spirit, anti-bourgeois and popular. He felt that if decoration was the sign of the bourgeois weakening of architecture, in its own way, the Casa del Fascio was a project where Pagano felt "there was a need for decoration that was resolved at the expense of the harmony of the project".[48] Abstract decoration, but decoration all the same. Giorgio Ciucci was right in affirming that by harmony of the project", Pagano refers, not to Benedetto Croce's theory of the stylistic coherence of all the parts, but what Pagano himself defined as the "morality of the work": a morality that should produce simple, straightforward, honest, exchangeable projects, in other words, projects that he defined as "current". The Casa del Fascio could be interpreted in many ways, but it was definitely not 'current'. Therefore, Pagano was an exponent of social realism, while Terragni was an exponent of elitist lyricism; in Zevi's words: architecture in prose as opposed to architecture in poetry. Until 1937, when he died, Edoardo

46. Letter from Pagano to Terragni, August 8th, 1940 (AGT 918).

47. According to Giancarlo de Carlo, Pagano was part of what could be defined as the internal opposing faction of Fascism and who signed up as a volunteer to fight in the war "to atone", as he felt Fascism had taken a completely different turn from its origins. They were members of the Mystical Fascism group, like Renato Guttuso, Antonello Trombadori, Mario Alicata, Carlo Doglio and Giulio Carlo Argan, intent on restoring a "purer" form of Fascism. Again, according to Giancarlo de Carlo who had spent a lot of time with Pagano during the war, the group of Mystic Fascists was formed at the Littorali, the Fascist University Youth Games, in which Bruno Zevi also took part. Giancarlo de Carlo and Franco Bunčuga, *Conversazioni su architettura e libertà*, Eleuthera edizioni, Milan, 2017, pp. 44-45.

48. Giuseppe Pagano, "Tre anni di architettura in Italia", in *Casabella-Costruzioni*, n. 110, February, 1937.

17

Persico, the co-director of *Casabella* with Pagano, was the mediator between these two positions. But Persico also often returned to the concept of "moral sentiments", blaming the weakness of Italian architecture on the lack of these sentiments. But his interpretation of expression was different from that of Pagano: it was not at all idealogical, but aesthetic, like that of De Santis: the balance between form and content. As a follower of Crocean philosophy, he knew that moral sentiment did not necessarily need to result in political action, but should be expressed as absolute dedication to one's own work, understood as a mission, in the same way Zevi was to consider the question later. After Persico's death, the disagreements between Italian Rationalist architects became far more defined.

In the 1930s, there was an end to what Terragni referred to as the "squadrista" period, when all worked together to oppose the monstrosities of Bourgeois architecture.[49] Naturally during that period, the split arrived in 1933, with the founding of the new magazine *Quadrante*, whose ideas were completely opposed to those of *Casabella*, directed by Pagano and Persico. Among the *Quadrante* editorial staff was the militant, Pier Maria Bardi, who had hosted the Second Italian Rationalist Exhibition in his gallery in Rome in 1931, and had created the renowned collage: "Table of Horrors"; with him were Bontempelli, Terragni, Belli, Figini and Pollini, and BBPR. If Casabella represented social, anonymous and current architecture, in opposition, as a fundamental value, *Quadrante* sustained lyricism and the indescribable nature of art. The objective of both magazines was to persuade the Regime, and thus the Duce, who made the final decisions on the choice of style with which the Regime would be represented. *Quadrante* was published for three years, and it was by no means coincidental that the last issue was entirely dedicated to what the editors considered a model for that style of architecture: Terragni's Casa del Fascio in Como. The magazine stopped publishing in 1936. This was not by chance. In fact, that year, the whole situation changed and the clash between Pagano's architectural prose and Terragni's poetry no longer had any reason to continue. That year, Fascism entered a new phase: the Imperial style. The war in Ethiopia the previous year and the relative international sanctions against Italy had pushed Mussolini and the King to declare that Italy was no longer a kingdom, but an empire; in short, a new version of the Roman Empire. With this new situation, architecture, the art

49. Giorgio Ciucci, *Gli architetti ed il fascismo*, Giulio Einaudi editore, Turin, 1989, pp. 105-107. Ciucci recalls what can be considered the lowest point in the relations between Terragni and Pagano, represented in a letter from Sartoris to Terragni in 1938, the year the racial laws were established, in which he wrote: "It is important to know if Pagano is Jewish. Find out, at any cost".

18

form of the State *par excellence*, would be transformed, just as it had been transformed at the time of Octavian Augustus: it too would become "Imperial". Until that time, Mussolini had followed various different directions as far as architecture was concerned, picking here and there among Classical, Rationalist, late Baroque and Ruralist styles, just as he had picked here and there in politics, whatever suited him at the time. The conflict among the various factions had been mitigated by the dividing up of the assignments and clever management by Piacentini, who still had eclectic tastes, undecided between Classicism and Modernism. With the establishment of the Empire, the Regime did something it had not done in the past; it decided definitively on its representative style, and chose to be expressed with stylized Classicism, with a metaphysical flavour, certainly not lacking in Modernity, also in stylized form. Colonnades, porticos, sequences of repeated openings, and stone cladding would have expressed the definitive stabilisation of the Regime. For the Rationalists, as Bardi stated: "all this was false modern monumental-academic", in other words, trash. With the change towards Imperial style, Pagano became closer to Piacentini, thus creating a rupture with the younger Rationalists. For some time Pagano and Piacentini had been sniffing the air, and had understood that a hypothetical alliance, or if nothing else, a calculated coexistence, would have brought advantages to both. As well, Fascist Classicism could probably have had something to do with that so-called simplified "current" architecture, clearly based on urban planning, that Pagano had in mind. The hypothetical convergence was still to be proven, and the testing ground was to be the project for the new University of Rome. Of the Rationalist group, Piacentini invited only Pagano, who designed his sober and elegant Physics Faculty. Pagano's decision to collaborate with Piacentini was seen by many Rationalists as a betrayal. A betrayal that was confirmed by another even more scandalous event. Pagano accepted to be a part of the limited group, made up of Piccinato, Vietti and Rossi, and led by Piacentini, who would design the project for the district for the Universal Exposition to be held in Rome in 1942. And that was not all. Almost as if wanting to consolidate the new alliance, with Piacentini and Valle, Pagano designed and built a characterless national pavilion for the Universal Exposition in Paris in 1937. After this experience, the relations between Terragni and Pagano deteriorated.

But in fact, Pagano realised that in the new Piacentini plan, there was no room for his social architecture; he understood that the celebratory colonnades would crush his 'current' architecture. He broke off with Piacentini, and from that moment, he began to attempt a reconciliation with the Rationalists, and in doing so, chose the most talented of the group, Terragni. Meanwhile, in 1937, almost as if wanting to give greater emphasis to his rupture with Piacentini, at the Milan Triennale, with Guarniero Daniel, he organised a photographic exhibition on Italian rural architecture; in other words, an exhibition on the most current, the most anonymous architecture possible, spontaneous buildings created by the rural classes, buildings without architects.[50] The exhibition was almost entirely based on photos that Pagano had taken himself with his Leika, travelling around rural Italy in search of its morphology and merits. Photographs of great quality, in black and white, where the shadows tend to stand out with a clarity that is clearly influenced by the Novecento style, and that can be compared with the photos taken by Terragni a few years later in Yugoslavia and Russia. Apart from the similarity between the two photographic styles, the differences are just as noticeable. While Pagano used a more rhetorical language, aimed at promoting the rural architecture that he had raised as a model in a return to the origins of Fascism, in Terragni's photos, this desire seemed to have vanished to leave room for a more intimate and inexpressible type of research. The strength of Pagano's photos all lay in their assertive academic eloquence; Terragni's photos were the opposite: elusive and evocative. Two different interpretations, for two different types of sensitivity, both emblematic of a debate that continued after the war without them. The fact remains that with the exhibition in 1937, Pagano and his photography launched the Neorealist movement that through its international success, managed to save the honour of a defeated and humiliated nation.

Despite their undeniable differences in the early 1940s, as often happens in the face of a common enemy, and in this case, Piacentini's group, Pagano and Terragni banded together and battled to reclaim Rationalist architecture. Giorgio Ciucci wrote: "The moment had come to think about a 'refoundation of architecture'. Terragni, Pagano and a few others were ready to take up the "battle for the cause of architecture". It was no longer the time for internal argument".[51]

50. For information concerning Pagano's photographs, see *Giuseppe Pagano. Fotografo*, exhibition catalogue edited by Cesare de Seta, Electa edizioni, Milan, 1979.

51. Giorgio Ciucci, *Gli architetti ed il fascismo*, op. cit., p. 194.

It was not the time for internal arguing, but neither was it the time for anything in general. The fate of the protagonists of modern Italian architecture had been determined. Before these events, Persico had disappeared in 1937. In him, Italian Rationalism had lost the most pro-European of its exponents, the least provincial, and the most resistant to the propaganda of the Regime. Because of his conviction and determination, he was extremely suitable as a leader for post-war Italian architecture. The rest was dictated by the war. In 1943, Pagano was forced to close *Casabella* and, repentant of his past, he joined the partisans. He was arrested, but he managed to make an adventurous escape, but was arrested a second time and sent to the Mauthausen concentration camp where he died from maltreatment the day before the Liberation. Persico died at 37 years of age, Terragni at 39, and the oldest, Pagano at 49. In an epitaph to Pagano, Zevi wrote: "The story of his life is part of the political and moral history of the finest among Italians".[52] This epitaph can be extended for the same reasons to Persico and Terragni.

In June, 1941, Terragni returned to Cremona from Yugoslavia, and was finally given leave to go back to Como. In his studio in via Indipendenza, one day he closed himself in the back room where he often worked alone, and without a pause, wrote his will.[53] He came out of the room and in his usual resolute style, he went to Zuccoli and asked him to accompany him to have it registered.
On the way home, they stopped at a café for a drink. Zuccoli recalled the moment, and spoke of Terragni being worried and undecided on what to do: undecided "this time for sentimental reasons".[54] Zuccoli made no other comments. Terragni's love life is not very clear. Terragni was a good-looking man, popular with women, and he enjoyed their company. With friends at the Polonio bar/café (called "La Mariett" after the owner) where he would go in the evenings, he would often make jokes and comments on the subject, even explicit and sometimes vulgar, even though Radice described him as being "shy with women".[55]
So, a big talker, but shy at the same time: yet another dichotomy in his character. But in 1933, he met who was to become his long-standing fiancée, Maria Casartelli, called Mariuccia. Zuccoli described how he and Terragni used to go to their usual bar/café, La Mariett, for a glass of "Punt e Mes", where they often saw an attractive brunette

52. Bruno Zevi, *Storia dell'architettura moderna*, op. cit., p. 277.

53. The will was published in Luigi Zuccoli, *Quindici anni di vita e lavoro con l'amico e maestro architetto Giuseppe Terragni*, op. cit., pp. 159-161.

54. The source of the news that followed was from Luigi Zuccoli, *Terragni militare. La guerra. Mariuccia Casartelli. L'immatura scomparsa dell'amico e il mio 1943*, in id., *Quindici anni di vita e lavoro con l'amico e maestro architetto Giuseppe Terragni*, op. cit., pp. 59-68.

55. Mario Radice, *Ritratto di Giuseppe Terragni*, in *Prima mostra commemorativa di Giuseppe Terragni*, exhibition catalogue, op cit.

19

already there but who would leave before them: "I often made some comment about her, but Terragni never said a word". One day, after one of Zuccoli's usual comments, Terragni told him to drop the subject and warned him: "Be careful what you say, she is my girlfriend". A girlfriend who was completely faithful and even devoted to Terragni. Zuccoli continued. "From that moment I was taken into their confidence and knew about their meetings, their silent walks around Como, trips to Milan, where Terragni would leave her at a café in Corso Vittorio Emanuele opposite Lingeri's studio, perhaps from 3 until 7 pm. Then he would bring her back to Como, maybe exchanging only a few words". When he left for the army, Mariuccia followed him to Cremona, and an irritated Terragni asked Zuccoli to discourage her. He wrote from the Firing Range in Nettunio: "I hope that the lady in question, who always wants to do things her own way, is in better health and does not have any plans for unexpected surprise visits as she did in Cremona. For now, she has not written a word. A pity".[56] Also emblematic is their relationship in the light of the letter that Terragni wrote to Zuccoli from Split in April, 1941: "I immediately wrote to Miss Mariuccia and I think my letter will reassure her. However, you need to let her know that it is very disheartening for someone far from home to receive news of that kind, so you need to do your best to prevent my having to experience this kind of situation again".[57] In 1941 when Terragni returned to Como from Yugoslavia on leave, he and Mariuccia had been together for eight years: at that time, it was unconventional not to have made some kind of decision about marriage. Several people close to Terragni, including Zuccoli, described how they had brought up the question of marriage many times but without any concrete results. So, it is probable that the 'sentimental reasons' to which Zuccoli alluded might have been provoked by another request from Mariuccia concerning marriage, a request that was becoming more insistent, almost as atonement for an absence that had now lasted over a year. This is a plausible theory; or after years of an engagement that did not seem to have been based on overwhelming passion, perhaps Terragni had fallen for some other woman in Cremona, Verona or Como. The fact remains that in his will, drawn up in June, 1941, Terragni left most of his property to his brothers, although he certainly did not forget Zuccoli ("to help pay his studies and start his professional architectural career") or his faithful fiancée.

56. Letter to Zuccoli, February 21st, 1941 (AGT 925).

57. Letter to Zuccoli, April 23rd, 1941 (AGT 927).

20

His bequest to Mariuccia could be interpreted as an act of love, or as repayment for his promise of marriage, shattered over the years by Terragni; or as an apology for infidelity towards a woman who had been faithful for so long.[58] Certainly there is little evidence to support this hypotheses, except for a letter, which was not even particularly erotic, that Terragni wrote during the early months from the Russian Front on September 30th, 1941, to a woman called Anna Lisa Ferrari, about whom little is known. Evidently in answer to a letter from her, Terragni wrote: "Unfortunately, my style cannot compete in such a literary field, because if it was already difficult before Russia, it has withered and wasted away in this incredible sequence of events during which we are learning to contemplate and evaluate everything without showing our emotions and feelings. If things continue in this way (a Russian winter is a wonderful experience!) I have the impression we will all become poets of the unexpressed, like Ciliberto. (Ask Luigi to explain in more depth!) Spiritual life is intense, but turned inwards, and very often it seems we have touched the very bottom; a new world seems to reveal itself in our febrile imagination. Then invariably, a shot from Russian artillery shakes us up and violently calls us back to our duty as soldiers, where in the end, we are really only boys who have grown a little and who are having fun playing at war. My warmest wishes to you and to our dear friend Luigi".[59] The letter is written in a tone that is both virile and introspective, between bravado and nostalgia, a tone that in some ways recalls Hemingway or Fenoglio when writing about the war. There is only one more allusion to other women, in a letter written by a certain Colonel Lerz. Terragni had returned from Russia, his mental condition was fragile, perhaps even damaged. To send him some comfort, the colonel wrote: "I am happy to hear that you have felt some improvement after the treatment by the Professors in Pavia. As soon as you can travel, come to Cremona straight away, and we will look after you and get you healthy again… here, we speak of you often and remember you fondly. You have to tell me the story about Tamara again! Remember?".[60]

Another complex relationship was that between Terragni and his Milanese business partner, Pietro Lingeri. They met in 1921 when Terragni was still a student at the recently established architectural faculty at Politecnico University in Milan. Lingeri, who was 10 years older, had already graduated from the Accademia di Belle Arti.[61]

58. The Terragni family told how, after Giuseppe's death, Mariuccia would often come to the studio to look at 'her' Giuseppe's paintings and photos.

59. Letter to Annalisa Ferrari, October 21st, 1941 (AGT 951).

60. Letter from Colonel Lerz from Cremona, March 23rd, 1943 to Terragni at the Neurology Clinic at the University of Pavia: "Dear Terragni, Excuse me, yesterday was the feast of San Giuseppe and I forgot to send you my best wishes. I have a lot on my mind and I did not remember. But, even if my wishes come late, please accept them all the same. I received your letter of March 17th. I am happy to hear that you have felt some improvement after the treatment by the Professors in Pavia. As soon as you can travel, come to Cremona straight away, and we will look after you and get you healthy again… here, we speak of you often and remember you fondly. You have to tell me the story about Tamara again! Today I am going to Fornovo because I have a group at the shooting and fishing school. I need to go because in June and July I need your help for the firing range/school we will set up in Clusone. When will we resume our project for the model barracks? Write and send me your news. I wish you luck and embrace you affectionately. Lerz (Colonel)". (Source, Terragni Archives).

61. Information on the relations between Lingeri and Terragni are published in: Paolo Nicoloso, "Lingeri e Terragni", in *Pietro Lingeri*, op. cit., pp. 59-75.

They began their first collaboration four years later in 1925, for the War Memorial in Como; after that, they worked together on nineteen projects, setting up their studio in Milan in 1931. Theirs was a long and profitable collaboration, although often contentious. Lingeri was well-connected in Milanese society, as was Terragni in Como. Lingeri possessed the diplomatic qualities that Terragni lacked, but Terragni had a rare talent and great determination; Lingeri was a competent professional, but Terragni's projects had a certain "something extra" that was lacking in Lingeri's work. Despite this, there were numerous reasons for the tension that existed between them, and during all the time they worked together, there were constant examples of resentment, disagreement, and small acts of retaliation. In the studio they shared in Corso Vittorio Emanuele in Milan, between 1933 and 1934, they designed several Milanese buildings (Casa Toninello, Casa Ghiringhelli, Casa Rustici, Casa Lavezzari and Casa Comolli-Rustici); later, with other architects, they worked on projects for competitions in Rome, like the Palazzo Littorio, another for the Palazzo dei ricevimenti, and the project for the Danteum. They also designed a project for the Trade Fair in Milan and the Library in Lugano. The first disagreements between Terragni and Lingeri were over the choice of the editorial team for the *Quadrante* magazine: Terragni supported Bardi, Lingeri wanted the Ghiringhelli brothers who had a more commercial and less radical perspective for the magazine. They were also excellent clients who had commissioned Lingeri and Terragni to design the apartment building in Milan that still bears their name. Thinking they had satisfied the debt of gratitude by assigning this work, the Ghirindelli brothers, who, it should be remembered had taken over the art gallery, Il Milione, from Bardi where they showed the work of the Abstractionists, decided to reduce their shares in the ownership of the magazine. Terragni did not appreciate this operation. The first disagreements began and developed during the drafting of the project for the new Brera Academy, changing their relationship. Terragni wrote in a letter in January 1940, that it was "a painful experience". It began with the difficult relations between Terragni and the other two prominent exponents of Italian Rationalism, Luigi Figini and Gino Pollini. In this conflict, Lingeri found himself in the middle; he tried to mediate, but only managed to worsen the professional relationship that he had with his difficult partner.

The situation developed in this way. In 1935, Figini
and Lingeri received the prestigious commission to design
the new seat of the Brera Academy. They involved their
respective partners, Pollini and Terragni, with whom they
drafted the project. It was approved by Mussolini in
December 1936, but was rejected by the "Superior Board
of Antiquities and Fine Arts" of which Marcello Piacentini
and Gustavo Giovannoni were members, who had evidently
decided to reject not only this specific project, but all Italian
Rationalist projects in general. After the rejection, Pollini
accused Terragni of being a shirker; of his own accord,
Pollini went to Rome to make the case with Bardi,
Bontempelli, Vadameri, Oppo and Pagano, and it was
Pagano who organised a meeting with Piacentini, at which
Lingeri was present, but not Terragni who was kept
completely in the dark about it. At the same time,
the controversy over the Casa del Fascio in Como arose,
where the proud, but thin-skinned Terragni was accused
of having copied his project from works like the Care Home
by Otto Haesler in Kassel, and the Vesna Women's
Professional School in Brno. A manifesto was drawn up in
Terragni's defence, which Figini and Pollini refused to sign
for fear of antagonising the academics with whom they were
negotiating admittance to the Brera Academy project.
Terragni, who certainly did not have a reserved personality,
considered their decision a harsh betrayal. Once again,
the Casa del Fascio triggered controversy and division, this time
between two companions from Politecnico University in
Milan and who in 1926, while still students, were among the
founders of the Italian Movement for Rational Architecture.
The controversy gradually developed into a professional battle
in which Lingeri seemed to side more and more with Figini and
Pollini. A far worse blow came for Terragni; Lingeri received the
commission for the artists' houses on Isola Comacina, without
telling Terragni, who was well-known in Como and was soon
informed of the fact. Terragni retaliated by participating in the
competition for the Arengario project in Milan with Antonio
Carminati and Giuseppe Mazzoleni, without including Lingeri,
who immediately replied by joining with Cattaneo, Origoni,
Magnaghi and Terzaghi in the competition for the Trade Union
Headquarters in Como, on the site adjacent to the Casa del
Fascio, winning the first prize. A bitter Terragni signed the
second project for Brera in which he had not participated.
Bardi tried to repair the relationship by assigning them both
the commission for the headquarters of the Fascist Glass

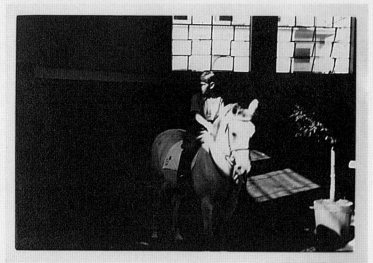

21

and Ceramics Institute in Milan, but a disgruntled Terragni, although he signed the commission, did not participate in the drafting of the project which suffered from Terragni's absence. In 1939, just before Terragni's departure for the army, despite Bardi's attempts at reconciliation, the professional partnership between the two seemed to be definitively in a deadlock. So it was no coincidence that Terragni decided to set up new alliances, breaking free from Milan to open a studio in Rome with Sartoris and Cereghini. In a letter written when he was in the army in Cremona, in January 1940, he decided to break off with Lingeri completely, proposing that they divide the commissions, in which he included Lingeri's personal projects like that of the houses on Isola Comacina, and the Trade Union Headquarters in Como. Lingeri, as usual, was diplomatic and evasive, and answered the provocation in accommodating and even compliant tones, in great part surrendering to the requests of his burdensome partner. His surrender was also part of a strategic vision of how the situation was evolving, knowing very well that with Piacentini's loss of influence and the new balance of power, antagonising Terragni would have precluded any possibility of Roman commissions which, as was obvious with the project for the Glass and Ceramic Building, seemed increasingly more probable. So a form of agreement was decided between the two, even though the Brera project was far from resolved. Just as they were trying to divide up the outstanding matter, the Brera Academy assigned a third commission, but only to Lingeri, who wanted to share it with the others once again. But Terragni did not want any more contact with Figini and Pollini, whom he considered as traitors to Modernist Architecture. An embittered Figini wrote: "Nobody (including Piacentini, Ojetti, Farinacci, and others) has mistreated us with such tenacity as has our colleague (!) from Como! Enough! this is one of the worst, in fact the most offensive meeting of my career". At the end of February, Terragni was granted leave and drafted the third project for Brera with Lingeri. Lingeri tried to intercede once again between Terragni and Figini and Pollini without success, and in May, when Terragni was granted leave again to control the plans for project submission, which he considered simply the completion of what he had drafted a few months before, he warned his partner not include the names of Figini and Pollini in the documents, placing Lingeri in a difficult position. The war, which broke out just at that moment, relegated the Brera

22

project and the split between Italian Rationalists into the background, until it disappeared altogether. As well as the professional squabbles and differences, a sense of rupture remained, typical of Terragni's inflexibility, which was rooted in his desire to preserve the integrity of Modernist architecture, (something Zevi insisted upon several times). Terragni felt this was compromised in projects like the building constructed by Figini and Pollini with Mario De Renzi at the E42; it was easy to see why a building of this kind would irritate Terragni. The conflict had embittered and disturbed Figini and Pollini, but as Terragni himself wrote to Mario Radice: "I would have liked more unity and cohesion in our efforts during the difficult struggle for our ideas. Perhaps I demanded too great a sacrifice of each individual artistic personality for the collective victory of the group. In any case, I don't feel I am guilty of having lacked faith in life and humanity in general".[62] Terragni's feelings can be seen in an affectionate and confidential letter sent to his trusted friend Zuccoli from the Russian Front, in which, rather evasively, he referred to his complex relationship with Lingeri.[63] In a rather paternalistic tone, Terragni advised Zuccoli to "distance himself" from Terragni so he would "not end up like Lingeri". He did not elaborate on the subject, as if Lingeri's subordination, even subservience with regard to Terragni, infused with a certain resentment and always ready to engage in some underhand conflict, was perfectly clear to him. It also seemed clear that he was aware of his own annoying character that sometimes came close to an abuse of power. However, more than the others, he felt he had a mission to fulfil for Modernist architecture, and those on a mission tend to trample the rights of others. The end of the relationship between the two partners was to be written in history. Shortly after Terragni's death, the terrible allied bombing of Milan destroyed Lingeri's studio. Many competition project drafts and working drawings they had created together were lost. The only ones that survived were the plans for the Danteum, that by accident, were not in the studio. The bombs also destroyed the Lingeri family apartment in the same building. The family found themselves without a home. Ironically, they moved to Como, in via Indipendenza, to the Terragni house, into the apartment that, shortly before, had been home to Michele (head of the family) and the youngest son Giuseppe who had just died.

Terragni's complex, multifaceted personality was by nature dualistic: on one hand was the swaggering,

62. Mario Radice, *Ritratto di Giuseppe Terragni*, in *Prima mostra commemorativa di Giuseppe Terragni*, exhibition catalogue, op. cit.

63. Letter to Zuccoli, March 10th, 1940 (AGT 930). In this letter, Terragni advised his collaborator to distance himself and accept work away from Como, a career, in which, as can be seen in other letters, Terragni took a direct interest. On hearing the news of Zuccoli's departure for other work, Terragni wrote: "...I am sorry, and this is normal, because of the strong affectionate friendship that we have enjoyed for 20 years. It is precisely because of my affection for you I want to encourage you, because, apart from the economic aspects, you also have the opportunity to move away from that stupid provincial environment that could damage your professional career in the future. In the same way, it could be detrimental for you to stay too close to me, as I have the impression I have been prejudicial for other people (Lingeri for example)".

23

64. Bruno Zevi, *L'Architettura. Cronache e storia*, op. cit., p. 272. Zevi wrote later: "This architect from Como is a difficult, troubled, heartrending individual. Despite the Fascist dictatorship, he creates democratic subversive buildings. Generally, he manages to avoid the rhetorical overstatement of the Classicist structures. His linguistic research is complex, it is not limited to the combinatorial application of source ideas from the maestri".

65. Luigi Vietti, *Un grande amico* in *Giuseppe Terragni. Opera completa*, op. cit., pp. 17-18. On the other hand, Alberto Sartoris wrote: "[...] Giuseppe Terragni was built like a rock, but he used his strength and violence only at crucial moments, to achieve a more stable equilibrium and great perfection. Generally, he preferred to prevail, convincing others politely, rather than taking advantage of his physical or moral dominance. However, when it was necessary to strike hard to save a desperate situation in extremis, he went in fighting, with strong dialectics and irrepressible passion". Alberto Sartoris, "Presenza di Giuseppe Terragni" in *Prima mostra commemorativa di Giuseppe Terragni*, exhibition catalogue, op. cit.

66. Ico Parisi, "Con Terragni", in *Giuseppe Terragni. Opera completa*, op. cit., pp. 9-12.

67. Luigi Zuccoli, "La conoscenza di Terragni", in *Quindici anni di vita e di lavoro con l'amico e maestro architetto Giuseppe Terragni*, op. cit., pp. 4-6.

68. Ignazio Gardella, "Un ricordo" in *Giuseppe Terragni. Opera completa*, op. cit., pp. 7-8.

69. In his portrayal, Radice also described some of Terragni's work methods: "In the many competitions which he entered, always with excellent results, his plans and those of his group always arrived at the last minute and with a hasty or incomplete presentation. During the turmoil before the competitions [...] he would isolate himself to do his research. He did more research than anyone else, he searched for rare books to collect data and references and, far more than the others, he analysed every investigation in depth. When the planned solution was completely ready in every detail, he was still not satisfied and would arrive with a new solution, even better. So, during the two days before the deadline, we had to start over again". Mario Radice, "Ritratto di Giuseppe Terragni", in *Prima mostra commemorativa di Giuseppe Terragni*, exhibition catalogue, op. cit.

talented, privileged, Futurist, ostentatiously anti-bourgeois personage, and on the other, the introverted, private, sometimes inaccessible individual, completely focused on his work, that he executed alone, often at night, as far away from others as possible. A duality reaffirmed by Zevi, who never actually met Terragni personally, but who described him in this way: "Giuseppe Terragni, an Italian with a desperate leaning towards the concept of Europe, blundering, yet sure and certain, complex but crystal clear, pragmatic and romantic: the other clean-cut side of Italy, and therefore, opposed to narrow-minded provincialism, and alone".[64] That is not entirely true. Terragni had never been alone, and certainly he was not opposed to "provincial towns", which was where he originated and to which he owed his professional success. There are many descriptions of him from people who knew him personally. Luigi Vietti wrote: "Terragni was a *maestro*, a charming man: tall, dark, not particularly handsome; he had a resounding voice, and he was very charismatic and persuasive; you were either with him or against him".[65] Ico Parisi, a Sicilian who moved to Como and worked for some time in the Terragni studio, becoming a recognised designer after the war, also commented on the duality of Terragni's personality: "Giuseppe Terragni was a complex individual: an extrovert, who alternated this open side of his character with moments of taciturn irritation; apparently lazy in the morning, dynamic and tireless at night. He liked to be surrounded by his friends, a small court that he dominated and tyrannized".[66] An impression confirmed by Zuccoli: "I knew him as a cheerful, pleasant, overbearing games companion, always sure of himself, successful, always ready to find a hundred pretexts, even the most ridiculous, to justify being beaten at cards or billiards".[67] The aristocratic Gardella found Terragni "very tough and aggressive"[68], while Mario Radice felt "that because of childish reserve, he hid his feelings behind facetious sarcasm, or, depending on the occasion, behind provocation and remonstration".[69] Another impetuous character like Terragni, Piero Maria Bardi, wrote: "Peppino was an imposing man, tall, strong, but well proportioned. He was hard-headed, with the same stubborn tenacity you might find in a giant, but he had beautiful eyes, and a kind, soft expression, even a little mysterious, like children have, and while the whites of our eyes became dull or red because of anger, or overwork, the whites of his eyes remained blue, and left a strong impression.

I mean, the colour was truly blue, sometimes unbelievable. His spirit seemed to be immersed in a heavy sense of tranquillity, but he was constantly ruminating, and when it flared up, it was powerful. He talked a lot, yet it always seemed as though he was almost quiet. The things he said were not especially significant, and yet, you understood that they needed to be said. Everything about him was necessary. Nothing about him was random, superfluous or gratuitous. His projects were always the faithful interpretation of this concision, and to escape this relentless pace, he would show an ethereal, lyrical flexibility that was another rather exposed aspect of his character: his childlike nature." And he added: "…very often, with another person, he liked to share the procedure he was applying to reorganise his ideas".[70]

This childlike aspect was reaffirmed by Mario Radice: "His stature and authority were in contrast with his expression which was reflective and candid like that of a child. He had open, friendly features, strongly marked, roughly traced, and had a deep voice. Amazingly, these heavy clumsy hands and a roughly sharpened pencil would produce slender strokes, very fine lines, sharp and vibrant. He would make some typically "Ambrosian" sharp-witted comment, and he was proud of the fact he had been born in the province of Milan; but he was not like the usual outgoing, talkative Milanese; on the contrary, he was a man of few words, sharp, concise and blunt, like people from the mountains". And he added: "His clothes were rather scruffy, and he did not have much time for people who considered it important to dress well. He had quite a disorderly lifestyle, although he would have preferred more order, which he never managed to apply. He felt that the hours spent sleeping were wasted; he would berate the friends who wanted to go home at midnight, but two hours later would give them a tongue lashing for making him waste time. He had a difficult, brusque character, and was literally impossible in the mornings, perhaps a sign of regret at having lost so many mornings. In fact, he got up very late, either because he had worked during the night, or because he was enjoying himself with friends and colleagues until the small hours. Everything in his studio was open and in full view of anyone who entered; he never kept a drawer closed, not even in his home, and often, he did not even close his door.

70. Pietro Maria Bardi wrote: "Terragni was as loyal a man as I have ever met; he was decent, honest, with great courage. I spent a lot of time with him, and when he came to Rome he almost always stayed in my home. He never stopped, and would never have stopped talking about architecture. He wasn't a great speaker, his arguments weren't laid out on a critical basis, he expressed himself more with gestures and exclamations than through deliberation. I often told him I always considered him the 'unwitting Comacine master'". Bardi added an interesting fact: "Terragni entered the Fascist movement in the same way you go to be vaccinated, without discussion and without reflection", Pietro Maria Bardi, *Il volto del secolo. La prima cellula dell'architettura razionalista italiana*, Pier Luigi Lubrina editore, Bergamo, 1988, p. 62.

His personal cubbyhole, where he liked to isolate himself, working until outlandish hours, was mainly occupied by a large table overflowing with cluttered papers, with a pile in the centre, two or three hands high, that slumped towards the edges until they hung over, drooping towards the floor which was strewn with other papers, pieces of marble, and other construction material samples, frames, paintings, and objects of every kind. He would sit at a corner of the table and draw wonderful sketches that were the basis for his projects. Awkward with women, and timid with talented artists, he was not at all reticent with powerful men who were wealthy or politically important, with whom he behaved in a surprisingly relaxed way, although coupled with secret aversion. But he did not know how to deal with clients because before any other subject, topic, or interest, his first priority was the beauty of the project design. He drove construction site suppliers crazy for the same reason […]". Radice paused to mention an important aspect: "Among his friends and the people he relaxed with, were famous artists, a cabinet maker, a millionaire and an apprentice barber; an important industrialist and a coffin welder; a state employee, a cabinet minister, and a milkman".[71] Piero Lingeri's portrayal of Terragni was more grandiose and deferential: "...Giuseppe Terragni: He immediately surprised us with his profound, lively expression, his unusual demeanour, almost inaccessible for us, fellow disciples. He was absorbed by the celebration of his destiny, seeming to emerge from a world of Michelangelesque spirits, pursuing bizarre architectural visions, alien to every circumstance and every sense of contemporary society. A haughty giant in a world of dwarfs, he opened his heart one day about the Comacine Masters, re-invoking ancient times when the master stone masons from the Lario valleys, travelled throughout Europe, expressing the original architectural spirit in the lightness of transfiguration. Like Sant'Elia, he felt the world was lacking in style; the harmony between mankind and form had faded, it was essential to draw from definitive primordialism the new sense that would restore the 'whole' into human terms. Certain foreign architects, from Le Corbusier to Gropius, agreed with his urge for radical renewal. He was the first among us to begin that architectural campaign that only death would interrupt... Troubled by an immense, complex imagination, in an eternal struggle with himself, through his daily efforts, Terragni managed to bring to light the pure form that represented the dawn of our Modernist architecture".[72]

71. *Giuseppe Terragni*, in *Prima mostra commemorativa di Giuseppe Terragni*, exhibition catalogue, op. cit.

72. *Pietro Lingeri*, in *Prima mostra commemorativa di Giuseppe Terragni*, exhibition catalogue, op. cit.

24

If we look beyond the prose, Lingeri did seem to seize Terragni's 'mystic' quality, his obstinate desire to belong to a mythical timeless realm which he perceived, but which others did not. Lastly, there is the statement by Ernesto Nathan Rogers who wrote the following comments in Casabella after Terragni's death: "Terragni was constantly tempted to inflate his architecture to adapt it to the language of the Regime; because of his own naivete, he did not perceive this weakness at the beginning, but then the recoil of his art pressed back incessantly, and gave him strength and fortitude, so that finally, his courage merged with the force of his style; this was the moment when, despite the contamination of Fascism, Italian architecture was saved, in an oasis of truth from which it will be able to continue its path without recanting [...]. Those who knew Giuseppe Terragni, "Peppino", certainly remember that his physical stature was the embodiment – or rather an allegory – of his spirit. One was immediately struck by the penetrating expression in his eyes set in that broad jovial Lombard face: his diffidence constantly in conflict with his exuberance (like the classical structural design of his constructions and his evasions into plasticism) or his rough and rowdy argumentative discussions, and his wary defensive position on the sidelines. Intelligent, but not especially well-read. He took risks, but was guided by his sixth sense, that instinct common to all true artists, which prevented him from falling over the precipice to which he was drawn by his curiosity, enthusiasm, and reckless spirit. His originality never depended on improvisation or eccentricity, because it was always rooted in tradition. He tried to translate the impossible slogans of the regime into artistic purity, but maintained his honest provincial position where, rather than the idea of a swaggering empire, in the end he preferred the concrete reality of his own town".[73] Many people all agreed on Terragni's complex and contradictory personality, just as they agreed on his charismatic appeal. In all, one has the impression of a man absorbed by his own character, but without vanity, completely committed to the surges of his personality, in turn dominated by his work, or rather, his mission.

In July 1941, Lieutenant Giuseppe Terragni left for the Russian Front. Before his departure from Cremona, on the first of the month, he wrote to his trusted friend Zuccoli: "In a few days we will be leaving the country and who knows

73. Ernesto Nathan Rogers, "Un monumento da rispettare" in Casabella-Continuità, n. 212, 1957.

25

how long it will be before we will come home. So, it is time for you to deal as quickly as possible and as best as you can with all the unfinished business that you are well aware of". As usual, the problems were mainly financial. In the letter he mentioned new commissions, but nobody had paid the previous projects or those underway, and this, while two of the three brothers, owners of the studio, were away at war. First of all, there was no payment from Mrs. Giuliani-Frigerio, the Municipality had not paid for the social housing project, and the financing for the Casa del Fascio in Lissone was also blocked. Terragni wrote to Zuccoli: "Wars are fought with l'*argent* (money), even from a personal point of view!", and added that the war was fought on two fronts, both military and architectural.[74] In August, in reply to Zuccoli who asked what he should do to move the commission payment problems ahead, Terragni answered in an ironic, sarcastic tone: "It would be a good idea to reply with some dark Russian humour: you can make a crack saying that I am away at war risking my skin, and so, since I am in need of all my skin, for that reason I have no intention of being "skinned" in Como".[75] In another letter on November 18th, when he had been at the front for some time, he wrote to Zuccoli again. He said that his brief mission in enemy territory had been successful, and hoped that the compensation promised for military action would not be reduced by 50%, "like the fees back at home!". The tone of the letter showed Terragni in a light-hearted mood, and if nothing else, confident. After all, in August 1941, to the Axis forces, the Russian Campaign seemed to be yet another proof of the resounding efficiency of the Wehrmacht Blitzkrieg. Operation Barbarossa, the invasion of the Soviet Union by the Axis forces, had begun on June 22nd 1941. Without any prior warning, Hitler had revoked the non-aggression pact he had established with the Soviet Union a few days prior to his invasion of Poland, which had launched the Second World War. During the months before the Axis attack, the troops were massed along the border: the numbers alone did not seem to leave any doubt as to their intentions. Stalin was not aware of this, convinced that Hitler would not open a new front in a war that was practically won. He was wrong: it was Hitler's intention to annihilate the Soviet Union in a short time to demonstrate the superiority of the *Übermensch* "Super Man" over the "Collective Man", and because he needed Russia's raw materials. The summer of 1941 was the propitious moment to "suddenly focus on the east".

74. Letter to Zuccoli, July 1st, 1941 (AGT 937).

75. Letter to Zuccoli, August 17th, 1941 (AGT 938).

26

The Führer was also convinced that the defeat and destruction of the Soviet Union would have created a new balance, forcing Britain to accept peace with Germany.

So, on June 22nd, 1941, a couple of weeks later than planned, due to the Wehrmacht having to pull out the Royal Italian Army from Yugoslavia where it had been bogged down, the Axis forces attacked the Soviet Union without warning, and 3,500,000 men, plus 3,500 tanks and 2,700 planes entered the vast Soviet territory. The Axis forces were mostly German, with additional troops from Romania, Hungary, and Italy under the command of the Wehrmacht. In theory, this deployment, which was predicted as the largest invasion in history, was to face an army of 4,500,000 men, equipped with a large number of tanks and planes: however these numbers did not take into account an exhausted Red Army devastated by Stalin's purges.

The first days of the invasion were tragic for the Soviets. Already during the early weeks, the Axis forces had destroyed a large part of the Soviet aviation, often while still on the ground, while the armoured troops marched into Soviet territory like a knife slicing through butter. Hitler's predictions that Operation Barbarossa would be won in less than three months seemed to be confirmed once again. Ukraine was defeated in even less time than predicted, and the Soviets, forced to beat a hasty and disastrous retreat, did not even have the time to blow up their bridges after they left.

During the dramatic days of the retreat, Stalin was nowhere to be found. He was hidden in his dacha, and only his closest collaborators knew where he was. On July 3rd, when the fate of the war seemed to be determined, Stalin reappeared with a speech on the radio that has gone down in history. In his address, the Georgian dictator spoke to his people without using the rhetoric of Soviet propaganda, but the language of Czarist and Orthodox tradition. He did not call his companions, but his brothers and sisters, whom he asked to make an ultimate sacrifice to save Mother Russia. Stalin's call did not go unheeded: over twenty million brothers and sisters sacrificed their lives for what Stalin defined so appropriately, the Great Patriotic War.

A month after the beginning of the attack, the Axis forces had penetrated 700 kilometres inside Soviet territory, completely defeating Ukraine and the lower Dnieper basin, with the cities of Kiev and Smolensk. By September they were at the gates of Leningrad and close to the last station on the metropolitan rail line to Moscow.

27

But it was also in September that General Žukov and General Tymošenko set out a plan for a strategic retreat, launching a surprise counter-attack that lasted until January 1942, in which the Red Army suffered enormous losses, but recovered 200 kilometres. Moscow was saved and despite being under harrowing siege, Leningrad resisted. In September, with a move that was to decide the fate of the war, Hitler transferred the front to the south and directed the Wehrmacht towards the Caucasus to capture the oilfields, in the hope that their possession would permit the troops to reunite with Rommel's Afrika korps to crush Egypt, firmly under British control. A month later, on October 3rd, 1941, in a public address, Hitler announced that following the fall of Kiev, the enemy on the Eastern Front was now crushed, and that behind the Wehrmacht outposts was a vast territory twice the size of the entire Reich. But on the road towards the south, on the banks of the Volga, was the city of Stalingrad, an important strategic hub towards which Hitler directed one of his best armies, the Sixth Army, under the command of General Von Paulus. Undeniably, Hitler's desire to attack a city with such a name became an obsession. He was convinced that by destroying the city named after the Soviet dictator, the war would be won, and not only in the Soviet Union. In the months prior to the siege of Stalingrad, the Axis forces were positioned along a vast front stretching from Leningrad to the Urals, and for months, the battles seemed less frequent, almost as if the war had been swallowed up in the vast expanse of the Russian landscape. These were the early months in 1942, and even though it was never announced explicitly, the timing of Operation Barbarossa, as it had been initially planned, seemed to have failed. Hitler did not seem to be discouraged. On the other hand, the Wehrmacht high command was very worried about the possibility of having to deal with a Russian winter, along a vast, logistically unmanageable front. They attempted to persuade Hitler to avoid the attack on Stalingrad, by sending the troops around the city directly towards the Ural oil fields, but Hitler adhered steadfastly to his convictions, and remained convinced until the end.

The attack on the Soviet Union by the Wehrmacht in June 1941 was decided by Hitler without consulting their Italian ally. Mussolini was woken in the night by a phone call from a German colleague who informed him of the attack after it happened.

28

It was said that after he finished the phone call, Mussolini swore against his blundering ally, accusing him of behaviour that Mussolini would not have permitted himself even with his servants. After the disastrous experience of the Italian Army in Yugoslavia, pulled out at the last minute by the Wehrmacht, Hitler was very dismissive of the Italian participation in the Russian Campaign, also because he felt Italy should have focused all its strength on the already problematic campaign in Africa. Mussolini did not agree. Some time before, he had given orders for an expeditionary force to take part in the invasion; Hitler himself had confided his doubts about the campaign privately to Mussolini, although not officially. With the news of the beginning of Operation Barbarossa, the Italian Army had one week to organise the expedition as best as it could. On July 10th, 1941, the Italian Expeditionary Corps in Russia (CSIR) left from Italian railway stations for Ukraine, where they arrived early the following month. Lieutenant Terragni was part of the forces and among the first to leave from Cremona. The CSIR consisted of about 65,000 soldiers to support the Wehrmacht; their role was to control conquered positions and eliminate the many pockets of resistance. Their equipment was extremely inferior to that of the Germans. For example, the transportation Corps of which Terragni was part, did not include means of transport for the troops, but only logistics vehicles for equipment. Despite this, only one of the many examples of the Italian Army's lack of preparation, the Wehrmacht advance was so victorious that the lack of preparation in 1941 does not seem to have weighed heavily on the Expeditionary Corps. The CSIR reached the vast area to be controlled between the Dniester and Bug rivers in late autumn 1941. It was a strip of territory over 250 kilometres long, placed between the Romanian troops to the north and the Hungarians to the south. The transfer from Hungary, and the successive advance into Soviet territory were very rapid, as described by Terragni in his letters. A large part of the advance by the Italian troops was made in German trains and lorries, a humiliating situation, that paradoxically, made Mussolini hope for some block in the advance so that the Italian contingency could recover a minimum of military dignity. Ico Parisi, who was also part of the CSIR described the advance: "A sea of sunflowers on endless horizons and skies full of clouds like whipped cream. We travelled for countless kilometres along dirt roads searching for an enemy that we didn't hate,

29

30

we didn't know, and like us, they didn't know why they were there. Dozens of kilometres of dirt roads, up and down, that with the first rains became a sea of mud. Lorries and trailers were blocked, sliding towards the centre of the hollow without any way of steering or stopping them. The battalion blocked in this way seemed like giant insects trapped in birdlime, thrashing around in a useless effort to escape. In the end, we had to wait for the fine weather, before we could leave again. The column of lorries and trailers created a snake of dust in the green sea of the Ukrainian plains. A few rare glimpses of peasants outside their *isbas*, watching us with sad, but understanding expressions of our common destiny. Thin faces, bodies wrapped in padded jackets, as still as scarecrows; they watched us pass by, without understanding the reason for the large black boats we were trailing noisily behind us, breaking the eternal silence. The most common and constant feeling among those fighting a war is "nothing". You are nothing, you know nothing, you see nothing. You have a yesterday that has slipped away, a today of survival, and a tomorrow that is less than certain".[76] Another similar description, written by the Italian Army memoralist, Manlio Francesconi, also refers to his enchantment with the vast landscape: "The steppe seemed like an ocean; an ocean of earth, vast and unchanging, endless, where the gaze was limited only by the line of the horizon. An ocean where the relationships between the rare man-made elements appeared transformed – poor villages, small isolated stations, rows of posts where it was impossible to see where they began or ended, – that was the natural environment; an ocean where everything seemed so distant that it appeared unreal and out of reach. It was not earth, physical earth, but the transfigured expansion of the earth. Everywhere there were signs of poverty and desolation; where there were no concrete traces, the feeling was clearly present, widespread and oppressive".[77] The descriptions by Parisi and Francesconi seem embodied in Terragni's photos: often taken from the train that we imagine as the only moving object in a bleak empty landscape, a sensation of suspension between heaven and earth, disquietingly enchanting. A landscape experienced by a man who had always lived in the more intimate Italian territory, where every space is dense with the signs of its local population, where the landscape changes every few kilometres. The artist in Terragni sensed the diversity of all this, and was fascinated by it:

76. Ico Parisi, *Foto a memoria*, Nodo libri, Florence, 1991.

77. Manlio Francesconi, *Russia 1943*, Edizioni Studio Tesi, 1983, p. 19.

from his photos one has the impression that this space was seen and experienced as a means to regenerate his own architecture, expanding towards infinity. And indeed, he wrote: "Here the panoramas are vast, and I have an urgent desire to photograph them".[78]

Lieutenant Terragni's displacements were retraced by Emilia Terragni through painstaking investigations, comparing various sources, because, like all letters from the front, his letters were controlled by military censorship to prevent giving specific geographical indications.[79]
At first, at the beginning of the operations in mid-July 1941, the advance of the Italian troops was very rapid and throughout the journey they suffered no Soviet attacks. On July 17th, there was a short stop at the Oligopol Command post, and on August 22nd, Terragni wrote to Zuccoli, probably from the town of Pervomaisk, that had been occupied by German troops before his arrival: "We are camped in a small town on the banks of the Bug River. We will be moving forward soon. A true war operation, travelling hundreds of kilometres at a time. The town shows very visible signs of the terrible fighting here a week ago (it was captured and recaptured by the Germans four times). Now most of the population has come back and the roads are crowded with Germans, Italians, Hungarians and Russians. A chaos of different languages; I swim and row because my cantonment is on the banks of the river inside a timber deposit abandoned by the Russians who fled". He added: "All in all, we live quite well in spite of the transfers by road (which are mainly only tracks and trails) that represent a real problem, especially for the logistics vehicles".[80] A few days before, in another letter dated August 4th, Terragni asked Zuccoli to send him some rolls of film as soon as possible (Terragni shot a large number of his photos during the advance operations). He asked for different types of black and white and colour film; he also asked for cinema film rolls.
In a successive letter, Terragni wrote that he had shot three short films, material that was lost, probably because of their precipitous and dramatic return to Italy. However, the fact that he asked for material of this kind is fairly indicative that the Italian advance at that stage was not yet under true war conditions. In the same letter, he made some comments that merit reflection: "If it ends as it began, this Russian Campaign will be a truly interesting experience, because

78. Letter to Zuccoli, August 17th, 1941 (AGT 938).

79. Emilia Terragni, "Gli anni della guerra nel carteggio di Giuseppe Terragni, 1939-1943" in *Giuseppe Terragni. Opera completa*, op. cit., pp. 281-293.

80. Letter to Luigi Zuccoli, August 22nd, 1941 (AGT 926). In this letter, Terragni asked Zuccoli to send the following: Laundry soap, cigarettes, rolls of film (he had already received some in the first package) and tobacco, warning his friend Zuccoli that he had started to smoke a pipe again.

it will confirm what I (and you too) have always maintained concerning the actual conditions in this country. Tell our overly conventional friends at Caffè Rebecchi!".[81] What did Terragni mean by "actual conditions" and "overly conventional friends"? It must be remembered he was writing under military censorship, and could not be as direct as his temperament dictated, however, despite this, the phrase seems to hint quite clearly that in Como, he and Zuccoli had already discussed the Soviet Union, probably speculating on conditions in the country as being different from the picture diffused by Fascist propaganda, and endorsed by their "overly conventional friends" in Como. After all, if there was an aspect of Fascism that Terragni supported, it was the grass roots movement, of the masses, if not "squadrista", it was a movement he intended as a *counter-melody* to Bolshevistic egalitarianism, to which in an indirect way, Fascism owed a great deal. It should be remembered that Fascist Italy was the first to recognise the Soviet Union in the League of Nations. Probably Terragni was attracted to the idea of a possible commonality between the two regimes, who knows? The fact remains that he was familiar with and admired Soviet architecture; there are numerous books on the subject in his library and his eccentric relations with the land of the Soviets were confirmed by many of Terragni's friends, first of all Bardi, who had travelled there, and on his return wrote a book with the eloquent title: *A Fascist in the land of the Soviets.*[82]

Meanwhile, in the autumn of 1941, the increasing loss of efficacy in the Wehrmacht advance began to have the first repercussions on the Italian troops. The CSIR halts en route became shorter; clocking up the kilometres of the steppe began to appear like something from another war, left far behind. In a letter sent on September 12th, 1941, Terragni told Zuccoli that he had experienced his baptism of fire; it was two years since he had been called up, and it was only now that he could see this war that he would not leave for another year. The baptism was aircraft bombings, and Terragni wrote that his unit had behaved "admirably". Since winter was approaching, he also asked for gloves, wool sweaters, "thick wool skier's socks", and "if you can find a fur lining… like the one our good friend Rho wears under his raincoat". He also asked for his beloved cigarettes, adding another request: "Another thing, and I hope this will make you happy, at least I hope so: I would

81. Letter to Zuccoli, August 14th, 1941 (AGT 959).

82. Pietro Maria Bardi, *Un fascista nel paese dei soviet*, Bollati Boringhieri, Turin, 2000.

like a small complete box of oil paints [...] and a box of pastels and coloured pencils, with a couple of sketch books and some Conté and Negro 9 sketching pencils for fairly smooth paper". And he added: "I have already done some pencil sketches and during any pauses in the war, I would like to develop this artistic inclination, because this is an intensely interesting country, and apart from photos, it would be wonderful to have some personal artistic reminders, to look back on years later".[83]
"Intensely interesting" despite the war. In September with the first signs of the Soviet counter-attack, Terragni had a second encounter with the enemy, this time directly. According to Emilia Terragni's research, between September 28th and 30th, Terragni's regiment was in the Petrikowka area, on the other side of the Dnieper. From there he wrote as usual to Zuccoli: "Three or four kilometres away, we can see the enemy artillery firing at us".[84] Probably he could also hear the relentless whistling sound of the Katyusha multiple rocket launchers, the noise that according to the memorialists like Rigoni-Stern or Bedeschi, would represent the sound-track of the defeat for the Italian soldiers.
In September, precisely when the war began to make itself felt, Terragni asked to be sent to the front lines. His request, unusual given the situation, was accepted and he was moved from the Field Corps Command behind the front lines to the 30th Artillery Battalion as a topographic surveyor, to take best advantage of his drawing capacity. As sarcastic as usual, he wrote to Zuccoli on September 28th, 1941: "as you can see from the address, now I am with the 30th. It was getting boring at the Command post, so I decided to come to the lines".[85] Mario Radice wrote: "Unfortunately he went to war in Russia. He was in heavy field artillery, which was not in the front line, but in the second, and he was in charge of his command unit, an infantry battalion. Naturally his friends and colleagues in the front line joked, calling him a slacker because the distance between the two lines was only three hundred metres [...]. In any case he was shielded from the front line, and he asked to fight in the front line with the artillery. That was where he performed his duty".[86] And yet at the beginning of winter he was still in good spirits. He wrote again to Zuccoli in November: I have had no news from you or from Italy for over a month. This is due to communication problems and unit operations moving around, and in particular, because I have even carried out some isolated operations with extremely brilliant results".

83. Letter to Zuccoli, September 12th, 1941 (AGT 939).

84. Letter to Zuccoli, December 4th, 1941 (AGT 947).

85. Letter to Zuccoli, September 28th, 1941 (AGT 940).

86. Mario Radice, *Ritratto di Giuseppe Terragni*, in *Prima mostra commemorativa di Giuseppe Terragni*, exhibition catalogue, op. cit.

His morale was still high: "I am becoming an old war wolf with my beard (not 'electric whiskers' yet, but not that sleepy either). Perhaps you don't know that I have an elegant black goatee beard that is the envy of all my colleagues.
On the other hand, the way this war is progressing, it is certainly not the right situation for growing a metaphysical beard.
We are very busy, and I have had the honour and risk of being engaged in reconnaissance missions in the areas still held by the Russians. This also earned me a citation in the daily bulletin. I ask you not to broadcast this around Como as you usually do".[87]

At the end of September, some unexpected news arrived from Como, no doubt through Zuccoli, about a new unspecified commission. In a letter on September 30th, Terragni replied: "Oddly enough, over the last few days I was just thinking about the possibility of designing some project, so I don't lose my routine completely; however, I would not have chosen some favourite project, but some small commission. And here, I have been given the opportunity by Engineer Venegoni [...]. Now that they seem to have organised a regular postal service (2 planes a week that land a few hundred kilometres from here) I think my contribution could be more than a simple consulting job. So it is up to you and Sartoris to organise this amazing collaboration, 2 or 3 thousand kilometres apart, with one foot in the war zone and one in peacetime".[88] In November in another letter, Terragni asked Zuccoli and Uslenghi (the studio engineer) for the survey information on the site, the commission requests, and news from Sartoris. He also asked them to thank Muzio, who was evidently involved in the operation. He thought that with the stable situation foreseen at the front during winter, he would have had the opportunity to work on the project, however he added: "But, if only you knew how far away the spirit is from these things!" Far away also because, in the same letter, he wrote that everything was lacking "in a country where there are no resources", adding "We live and fight in a territory where all storehouses have been systematically destroyed, so it is impossible to find goods of any kind. As well, there are no military commissaries, and comfort item rations are reduced to a minimum, when they have not been abolished completely. A large portion of the things sent from Italy goes missing or is tampered with: only one package in five reaches us!".[89] Meanwhile, the studio in Como was empty. Giuseppe's brother, Engineer Attilio, who had been

87. Letter to Zuccoli, November 11th, 1941 (AGT 944).

88. Letter to Zuccoli, September 30th, 1941 (AGT 942).

89. Letter to Zuccoli, November 18th, 1941 (AGT 945).

the Podestà of Como until a short time before, was away in Rhodes where he was commander of the Italian garrison. The other brother, Alberto, was also away at war, returning to Como shortly after with the grade of major.[90] Only Zuccoli remained, struggling at a time when nobody was paying the outstanding bills, and all probable commissions seemed to have vanished. Meanwhile in Russia, between October and November, the CSIR continued to advance as far as Donets, an industrial area with a number of coalfields abandoned by the Russians. The slag heaps formed huge striking black hills, symmetrical pyramids that Terragni sketched in his typical personal style, where he managed to combine Mario Sironi and the Constructivists, Sant'Elia and hermetic poetry, de Chirico and Bauhaus. Once again, Terragni was unfathomable: we do not know whether the person who took these photos felt, as we partly feel, the desolate image of decommissioned factories and bombed buildings, or whether they are little more than the desire to provide an illustration of the advance guard and the epic industries that had sustained them. Despite the fact that Terragni was a decisive man, sharp and categorical in his speech and behaviour, once again the atmosphere remains suspended, an enigmatic expression awaiting a meaning.

Suspended image was the title of the fine book that, in the early 1970s, Paolo Fossati dedicated to Lyrical Italian Abstractionism. Terragni was one of its main exponents because of his capacity to suspend the image of a building until it existed in an atmosphere where reality seemed to relinquish its presence.[91] Other suspended images were the enigmatic photos of the vast rarefied Russian landscape: suspended in a void where elements were re-signified, and then, an abstract composition would appear, like the photo where a passing plane on the left is balanced by a house floating in the steppe; or another photo where dirt roads form a supremacist cross, unwittingly walked over by a soldier. Even more alienating are the images of absolute emptiness, where now and then some trace appears in the landscape, like a dry stone wall, or the weave of crop stubble, faint and almost indiscernible, like the fine lines in Terragni's sketches. To balance the indefinable nature of the suspended images of the land, are the few but significant photos Terragni took of the Russian population, especially the peasants.

90. Terragni to Zuccoli in 1942: "I received a letter from my brother Alberto, who told me his injuries have prevented him from leaving for Russia, at least for the moment. He has done so much for the country during the war, and he deserves a bit of rest. Meanwhile he can show off the diamond on his Major's stripes around the streets of Como and Milan!" Letter to Zuccoli, July 21st, 1942 (AGT 951).

91. Paolo Fossati, *L'immagine sospesa. Pittura e scultura astratte in Italia 1934-1940*, Giulio Einaudi editore, Turin, 1971.

In one image, a family is coming out of its *isba*, walking towards the photographer. This is a moving image, probably an unconscious act of accusation against war, and at the same time, a loving gesture towards the poor and oppressed, recollections of descriptions by one of Terragni's favourite authors, Dostoevsky[92]. Just as in his painting and his architecture, in his photography too, the different personalities of Terragni seem to be laid on top of one another, eluding their inconsistency. By overlaying them, the personalities of the author appear like a watermark; an author who transfigured Modernism in his own personal way, drawing it through the past, through the poor and oppressed, the enigmatic and mysterious, through passion and melancholy.

In the autumn of 1941, after the defeat of Donetsk (named Stalino between 1929 and 1931), the CSIR was permanently deployed on the Don for a period of respite while the Wehrmacht outposts opposed the sporadic and destabilizing counter-attacks by the Red Army. The Italians, along with the Romanians and Hungarians, had the feeling they were experiencing a war in second place. Given the circumstances, Terragni had time to draw and paint, and most of all, he had time to reflect on his life. He was almost forty, far away from the place where he was born and had spent his whole life; a place to which he owed his fortune as an *enfant prodige et terrible*, highly talented, pampered by certain situations and events, but at the same time, he was very hard on himself, even intransigent, as can be seen with his choice to be transferred to the front line, so he would not "be bored". On October 21st, he sent Zuccoli an uncharacteristic letter. Unlike his previous letters, the tone was confidential; for the first time he treated his trusted assistant as a person with whom he could share his personal feelings. Terragni wrote: "I am writing from a town that could be anywhere in this vast Russia – I am lodged in a silo (not the vertical kind, thank goodness, but inside a long, spacious and well-ventilated hangar that provides a shelter for troops and officers (including the colonel); it gives the exact impression of a typically Russian Dostoevskian *Poor folks* inn. Outside it has been raining for a couple of days: the tracks have become a sea of viscous, black mud. To use a military term, we are magnificently bogged down; hundreds, maybe even thousands of vehicles are scattered and blocked for dozens of kilometres, a whole division stuck in the mud. We left xxx [sic] suddenly in a hurry to rush after the Russians who were

92. According to witnesses, Terragni had three favourite authors: First of all, Dante Alighieri, then Dostoyevsky, and Plato. There is an episode that contradicts Terragni's reputation as not being especially well-read. Bardi described how Terragni had explained certain concepts such as the root of irrational numbers in Plato's Theaetetus and Timaeus. Pietro Maria Bardi, *Il volto del secolo. La prima cellula dell'architettura razionalista*, op. cit., p. 63.

31

beating a retreat after the conflicts of the past few days, in which I had the pleasure and honour of taking part. In those unforgettable days I got to know some extraordinary commanding officers who enabled me to experience some exceptional moments. Now, I am forced to stay in an absolute deadlock as we wait for a couple of days of wind or a good frost that will let us extricate ourselves and start the chase again, or take the road to the sea. I can hear you asking my impressions of the war and its effects on the state of mind of an artist (that I honestly consider myself to be), in experiencing so many strong emotions that are so distant from the spiritual activities that an artist is normally involved in. It is very hard, in fact, impossible, to put into words the mass of emotions I have accumulated in these three months. Moments of extreme happiness, a wonderful feeling of detachment from things of this world, followed by plunging into the chaos of small daily hardships. Past life appears clear and limpid, recollections like a series of short film clips, most of all memories of childhood and adolescence. Our imagined and desired future lives are like a contrast with our past lives, and we make wonderful projects and programs (for the future). We plan down to the finest detail what will be a typical bourgeois day on our return (I confess that work occupies a very small part in the days we imagine). The worst sorrow we feel during these days, when there may be no tomorrow, is the regret that we did not make the most of all the good and bad things in life. Many (or rather most) of my fellow soldiers think only of going home to their families and the bourgeois lifestyle they were dragged away from. Not me. You know that and can imagine my feelings. I did not leave the so-called *riches* that the others had at home with their families etc. I did have them, and did enjoy them greatly, but now I am excluded and this places me in quite a different relational situation. I have very few friends left with whom I can indulge in this kind of conversation now and then".[93] This self-analysis almost seems to somatize the landscape or the war that surrounds him. Terragni's words resemble those of one of the most famous memoralists of the Russian Front, Mario Rigoni Stern, who, at the same time and in the same place, wrote: "Then the war arrived, the real war, right in the very place where I was, but I didn't feel the war, I felt intensely the things I was dreaming, that I was remembering, and that seemed to be more real than the war. The river was frozen, the stars were cold, the snow was glass that melted under

93. Letter to Zuccoli, October 21st, 1941 (AGT 943).

83

our boots; death, cold and green, was waiting on the river, but inside me, I had a warmth that melted all these things".[94]

In November and December 1941, the previous quiet period for the CSIR was over. In a letter on November 28th, Terragni wrote to Zuccoli: "I am writing in a hurry because the Russians are not leaving us any more time. I can't include the grenade blasts in these lines, but I assure you we can smell the stench, and it is very close. This war goes against all the predictions: the closer we get to winter, the livelier it gets".[95] And once again, in another letter to Zuccoli: "Dear Zuccoli, here, you have to learn how to wait and be patient! A fast-moving war! That's a joke! But we will win in the end. The main thing is to hang in there, compromise is for those who don't have faith in themselves and a victorious conclusion! I hope to come home in August or September".[96] And in fact, Lodovico Barbiano di Belgiojoso, who met him on the Russian Front during those days, described a buoyant Terragni, who was not at all worried about the current situation.[97] It is true that during the war Terragni did not lose his argumentative verve and hurled himself once more against the despised "pious Ojetti", the critic who had always been hostile to the young Rationalists. He wrote to Zuccoli that as a sign of contempt, he had brought with him to Russia the books of Gropius, Le Corbusier and Moholy-Nagy: evidently just as strong as his faith in a victory was his conviction that Modernist architecture was still "rock-solid".[98] Towards the end of 1941, he also read the book by his disciple and fellow citizen, Cesare Cattaneo, *Giovanni e Giuseppe dialoghi di architettura* and found it "crammed with ideas and concepts, great analyses and dissections of emotions and feelings".[99] But he added: "It is perfectly accurate, but a little too pedantic and too concerned with inventing a new multidimensional solution. The word is too long and incomprehensible, certainly more ambiguous than the definition so disparaged by fashionable artists: 'Rational', which, modesty aside, I chose personally as the insignia of the battles fought by our group way back in 1926".[100] These lines reveal the same customary Terragni, stubbornly asserting his claim that he was the heart and soul of true Rationalism, not the form compromised by the rhetoric of a Regime, in which paradoxically he believed, perhaps more than the others. At the end of 1941, the CSIR concluded its offensive with the battle of Chazepetowa where the new front was established.

94. Mario Rigoni Stern, *Il sergente nella neve*, Giulio Einaudi editore, Turin, 1965, p. 49. ("The Sergeant in the Snow" Northwestern University, June 1998).

95. Letter to Zuccoli, November 28th, 1941 (AGT 946).

96. Letter to Zuccoli, July 19th, 1942 (AGT 954).

97. Luca Lanini, "Commento", in Luigi Zuccoli, *Quindici anni di vita e di lavoro con l'amico e maestro architetto Giuseppe Terragni*, op. cit, p. 150.

98. Letter to Zuccoli, January 12th, 1942 (AGT 940).

99. Letter to Zuccoli, January 24th, 1942 (AGT 941).

100. Letter to Zuccoli, January 24th, 1942 (AGT 942).

On December 29th, Terragni wrote: "Dear Zuccoli, I am a few days late in writing because I have been very busy rebuilding and setting up our post for the long winter season of this incredible war (even if it is bleak), but which will find us stronger than ever in the spring. I have just spent about three weeks on the front line with one of our divisions. We occupied three quarters of the city and the rest was in enemy hands. Counter-battery fire: a true duel with the code of duelling, I shoot first, then you shoot, and so on. In any case, the shots surrounded us amiably and their noisy symphony accompanied us as we went to sleep in rooms requisitioned from the local population, who despite everything, have remained in the line of fire. Every morning, we calculated the progress or success of the enemy artillery which had adjusted their fire in our direction. I spent a calm happy Christmas with my comrades (perhaps better than in recent years)".[101] A good Christmas, during which he drew numerous sketches for the first Combat Artists' exhibition. It is easy to imagine that the working conditions must have been very insecure. There is a photo, evidently taken by one of his companions, that shows Terragni with his usual nonchalance, a cigarette hanging from the corner of his mouth, getting ready to work on a board outside an isba. Probably in these rather theatrical conditions of a Futurist at war, he drew large charcoal sketches showing soldiers talking or in war scenes.[102]

The sketches were sent to Rome, but did not reach their destination. In a letter to his brother Attilio, Terragni said he had delivered them to the painter, Castellucci, who was also in Russia, and had also been invited to take part in the exhibition. When Castellacci returned to the front he said that the sketches had not been exhibited because they had arrived too late. This was a straight-out lie, emphatically contradicted by the fact that Castellucci's drawings, which had been sent with those of Terragni, were put on show. An irritated Terragni wrote from the front: "Castellucci came back to the CSIR Command post a few weeks ago. I spoke to him as he deserved. He justified himself, talking about disagreements and arguments between Sapori and Marinetti. I find this strange, and in my opinion should not concern the possibility and (intrinsic) obligation to exhibit documentary works by an artist, who, on their invitation, assumed the often difficult responsibility of contributing to the glory of CSIR soldiers and their war".[103]

101. Letter to Zuccoli, December 29th, 1941 (AGT 945).

102. The incident of the sketches was reconstructed by Emilia Terragni in "Gli anni della guerra nel carteggio di Giuseppe Terragni, 1939-1943" in *Giuseppe Terragni. Opera completa,* op. cit., pp. 289-293.

103. Armed forces post card from Terragni to his brother Attilio, July 22nd, 1942. Source: Terragni Archives. Personal correspondence 1942; 8/1/7.

32

Seeing the prints of these drawings that have been handed down to us, the laudatory military intentions of the artist are obvious. They show cold, frozen scenes that transform heroic 19th century poses into sketches of everyday routine in the bold, virile style of 1950s film posters. Probably that is even how Terragni saw himself in the freezing Russian winter, in a war that went ahead in fits and starts, interrupted by long pauses in the frozen landscape of the Don. The enemy appeared and disappeared with a regularity that, over time, assumed a certain routine. Despite the failure of the first delivery for the Combat Artists exhibition, at least five of the fourteen sketches reached Rome and were later recycled for another showing on the same subject, but this time an international exhibition, to be shown in different European cities under direct or indirect Nazi control: Munich, Berlin, Vienna, Budapest and Bucharest. From Rome, the other nine were sent to Como, where thanks to the intervention of one of Terragni's closest friends, the painter Manlio Rho, they were shown at the Fascist Union exhibition in September, 1942. Brushing the compliment aside, Terragni wrote: "I do not deserve the honour paid by Como to my poor drawings. Thank Rho on my behalf, because all the credit goes to him. However, it was not necessary: Como is so far from here, and from me as well".[104] In his letter to Zuccoli, Terragni seemed to be in a different state of mind compared to a few months previously: downcast, and well aware that another winter in Russia was making him increasingly more isolated from his town and his country. Of the drawings exhibited in the European cities, only one image from the German catalogue remains. Once returned to Rome after the exhibition, they could not be handed back to the artist who had died in the meantime, and the efforts to recover them after the war by his brother Attilio, by then a Senator of the Republic, were in vain.

On May 26th, 1942, in answer to a letter from an apparently despondent Zuccoli, Terragni wrote: "I received your letter of May 7th, so full of discouragement and uncertainty. That is the way life goes, grey and dismal until the blue skies return. In the end, army life is not so very different from our normal bourgeois life. We have to learn to be patient… the lawsuits and the assignments are proceeding as I expected: it is a kind of Eastern Front for them as well! No joking… don't talk to me about the "fast-moving" war! But the day of victory will come for them as well".

104. Armed Forces post card from Terragni to Luigi Zuccoli, September 30th, 1942. Source: Terragni Archives, personal correspondence.

33

Then he added: "Here we are expecting a strong offensive: our section is working at full pace on the CSIR front and we are expecting new divisions. We are hoping to come home in August or September".[105] In the spring of 1942, for the last time, Terragni was still hopeful, to the point of making new plans for his return, speculating on the idea of publishing a register of his projects, like Le Corbusier: "I wrote to Engineer Olivetti at Edizioni Ines, about the publication. You and Uslenghi need to take care of all the material to offer Argan. However, this is a sensitive issue".[106] Olivetti and Argan: two names that were to become very important in the post-war period and who represented an expansion in Terragni's strategic alliances; for the first time he seemed disposed to disengage himself from the closed circle of Italian Rationalists. But he was mistaken (about the war), and in July, the Italian advance began again: "Dear Zuccoli. I will write a longer letter later when I have more time. We are involved in astounding advance operations and are bringing them to a victorious conclusion. We have already moved beyond two fortified lines and early tomorrow we will begin the charge towards the east".[107] It was an illusion. The Red Army was retreating to draw the unsuspecting Italian Royal Army into a zone that was far more suited to an attack by the armoured troops that the Soviet Army was determined to use even along the lengthy front of the Don. On August 20th, when the Italian Army was established on the west side of the Don, the Red Army attacked. This was the first battle of the Don, and lasted about ten days, putting a severe strain on the Italian troops who found it extremely hard to maintain the front line. Despite the situation, Mussolini continued to seem more worried that the Wehrmacht would outshine the Italian Army, than he was about the Red Army attack, an arrogance that often reached the point of tyranny. Against the advice of General Messe, the careful and realistic CSIR commander, Mussolini decided to implement the Italian forces in Russia by transforming the expeditionary corps into an authentic army: ARMIR (the Italian Army in Russia). In addition, the Germans, who were having problems in several units, and who were close to sending a large percentage of their troops to Stalingrad, began to demand additional Italian troops more or less explicitly. Mussolini explained the reasons for his choice to Messe: "Dear Messe, 200,000 ARMIR troops will carry more weight than 60,000 CSIR troops at the peace table". Naturally, Mussolini's words implied a rapid victory. In his mind, the plan seemed infallible: Stalingrad would fall without

105. Letter to Zuccoli, May 26th, 1942 (AGT 953).

106. Ibidem.

107. Letter to Zuccoli, July 19th, 1942 (AGT 954).

34

difficulty, and in the meantime, Italy would have expanded its commitment in Russia to gain greater political influence during the dividing up of Soviet resources. After that, once the Russian Campaign was concluded, the ARMIR troops would be redirected to North Africa. Despite the extraordinary military capacity of General Rommel's Afrika Korps, the Axis troops were in danger of having to surrender to the British Army, superior in numbers of men and equipment. So in June 1942, the CSIR ceased being a part of the 1st German Army and was incorporated into the 8th Italian Army under the name of the 35th ARMIR Army Corps. In spite of the increased troop numbers, the Italian Army remained in a support role for the motorised German troops, with the task of creating a defence buffer against Soviet counter-offensive attacks. This was a role that was suited to Italian units since, on the front along the Don, the Red Army was not yet using the armoured vehicles that would later smash the Italian, Romanian and Hungarian armies who had none of the same equipment. On August 23rd, 1942, the Italian troops answered a Soviet attack in the Izbushensky steppe with the victorious charge of the Savoia Cavalry. This was the last Italian Army cavalry charge, and was emblematic of the whole situation: the war, and the atrocious modern warfare using armoured tanks and air attacks, arrived only at intervals where ARMIR was operating; this underestimated war situation led to multiple mistakes by the Italian command, convinced that they would be able to deal with the foreseen increase in Soviet military capacity.

It did not take Terragni long to realise that with the arrival of the ARMIR, all his plans for returning home were at risk.

In a letter on September 5th, 1942, he wrote that he had seen large numbers of *Alpini* Mountain Troops: at first he thought they were replacements, then his illusions were dashed.[108] Captain Terragni had a short break in October when he was sent on a mission to Bucharest. From there he sent Zuccoli a post card showing a Mendelsohn style Rationalist building, and on the back he wrote: "I am on a short service trip to the distant Romanian rear lines. It seems like a dream after 15 months at the front. I am like a fish out of water, but I can still remember Modernist architecture. I am sending you an example".[109]

At the end of October, Terragni was still in the front lines and on November 28th, he wrote a letter to Sartoris, and seemed even more worried and discouraged. Then there was no more news, either to Sartoris or to Zuccoli, who, by this time, had been called up.[110]

108. Letter to Zuccoli, September 5th, 1942 (AGT 956).

109. Post card from Bucarest to Zuccoli, October 18th, 1942 (AGT 962).

110. Emilia Terragni in "Gli anni della guerra nel carteggio di Giuseppe Terragni, 1939-1943" in *Giuseppe Terragni. Opera completa*, op. cit., p. 291.

35

Until now, the only letters we have any information about, are those sent to a ten year old child, Luciano Guggiari, Terragni's godson. Three letters that have been carefully preserved by the family. The first was sent on January 24th, 1941, and the last, on April 1st, 1942, a few days before the new ARMIR troops arrived, at the time when Terragni still hoped he would be able to finally go home. Using simple language suitable for a letter to a child, Terragni wrote in answer to a package sent by the Guggiari family, saying that in spite of the discomfort and the danger he was happy to be seeing "very interesting things and countries".[111]

On July 3rd, 1942, the Wehrmacht began the siege of Stalingrad, and this decided the fate of the war, not only in Russia. The German troops' concentration on Stalingrad meant that the long front line with the Italians in the centre, the Hungarians to the north, and the Romanians to the south, found itself undefended, without any protection from the German armoured tanks which were now converging on the city on the banks of the Volga. The German command realised that the front along the Don, held by the Italians, Hungarians and Romanians was weak, and proposed a reorganisation in "whale bone" formation. This involved alternating the few remaining German armoured units with the allied troops, not taking into account the nationality of the oversensitive Italians who did not accept the plan, considering it did not respect their military autonomy. This was a rather temperamental decision, but one that did not worry the Wehrmacht command very much. However, it resulted as fatal. In addition to this strategic mistake, the Italians committed another error, partly justified by the lack of available troops. With the ARMIR units, they sent the Alpini Mountain Troops who were trained and equipped for mountain warfare, and certainly not suited to the vast flat Russian plains. The top Italian command had calculated the difficulties the Mountain Troops would encounter on the front along the Don, but they too were ill-informed on the actual military capacity of the Soviet Army, and thought that the problem would be resolved after the fall of Stalingrad when the mountain troops would be sent to the Caucasus mountain area as high quality support for the German troops. But from the very beginning of Operation Blue in July 1942, and the start of the siege on Stalingrad, General Von Paulus realised that the Soviets were willing to sacrifice themselves to defend their city. Resistance increased as the German troops penetrated

111. Source: Terragni Archives, personal correspondence.

36

the town, taking streets that were then lost again the following day in an exhausting alternating strategy that was completely new for the Wehrmacht which, till then, had only experienced incisive victories in open battle fields. In the city streets, almost completely destroyed, the German armoured tanks were no longer invincible; on the contrary, they were almost a hindrance when facing an obstinate, unassailable, heroic enemy, willing to fight hand-to-hand battle, and who followed Stalin's order to the letter: "do not surrender a single metre to the enemy". Hitler was furious. He could not understand how the Sixth Army, one of the best trained and best equipped, was not able to beat an enemy whom he considered not worthy of even being considered such, and he impulsively ordered them to advance, and not to retreat to the other side of the Volga, as good military judgement would have dictated, with winter on their doorstep. In November, at the moment when, for the first time, resistance seemed categorical, the head of the Red Army, General Zhukov, came up with an unpredictable, audacious, almost crazy strategy: he concentrated his troops in the north of the city where the Romanian troops were deployed, convinced they were safe in the middle of the steppe.

Within a short time, the 15 Red Army divisions, supported by their surprising T34 tanks, conquered the fragile Romanian troops. Unexpectedly, the Soviets did not attack the enemy in flight, but continued towards the south-west to the town of Kalach-na-Donu, behind Stalingrad, where they arrived very rapidly. At this point, the Red Army plan became clear: they would encircle the city on the west with their armoured tanks so that the besiegers found themselves under siege. As soon as the Germans understood the strategy, they set up a huge air lift to supply the 250,000 soldiers fighting in the city in an attempt to conquer the impregnable industrial sector in the north of the city. The air lift seemed to work for most of December, but the Soviet troops, perfectly at home in the freezing winter conditions, became increasingly more determined, and began to split up the German divisions who were finding it much more difficult to converge on the distribution centres for food and military equipment. The situation became critical the following month and Von Paulus increased his calls to Hitler in an attempt to convince him that a strategic retreat to the other side of the Volga did not represent a defeat, but simply a pause, if only to ward off the effects of a winter that was extremely harsh, far more rigid than the previous year.

37

38

Hitler refused and persevered with the attack on the industrial section. While a few city blocks heroically resisted the encirclement, whose very wide radius could not be detected by the Germans, the siege continued relentlessly, relying on the new tanks supplied to the Red Army which were discovered to be even better than the Panzer tanks which had been considered unbeatable until that point. With the failure of the air lift and the closing of the encirclement, in a short time the Battle of Stalingrad became a clamorous success for the Red Army and the Soviet troops attacked the Wehrmacht soldiers with the same ferocity that had been previously used against them. Encircled and starving, with few munitions, on February 2nd, 1943, the troops of Von Paulus unconditionally surrendered to the Soviet Army, which took 250,000 prisoners, of whom only a few would return home at the end of the war. A few months earlier, in November, with the Battle of El Alamein, the British Army had definitively chased the Axis armies from North Africa. In only a few months, the fate of the war had been completely overturned.

The Red Army attack against ARMIR is historically recorded as the Second Battle of the Don, and was launched at the same time as the Stalingrad counter-offensive on December 11th, 1942, just before Christmas. During the attack, this time the Soviets used armoured tanks that the Italians had never seen, and against which they had no equipment. Behind the relentless tanks, and protected by their aviation, were the Siberian troops, extremely competent and trained to fight in temperatures around thirty degrees below zero. The attack was deadly, and fought in parallel all along the front (about 200 kilometres) where the ARMIR to the north, and the CSIR to the south, were deployed. Initially it seemed that the Alpini Mountain Troops to the north would resist; More fragile were the placements of the CSIR where Terragni was positioned. Realising that the Italian front to the south was weak, the Soviets focused all their efforts there and on December 18th, two days after the beginning of the offensive, they launched a very violent attack. To avoid becoming encircled, the CSIR retreated rapidly towards the west, while the Italian troops to the north maintained the front line. But the mountain troops were no longer protected by the scarce German tanks, and to the north, the Hungarian troops scattered rather conspicuously. After resisting bravely, but with the danger of becoming encircled, the Italian troops also decided to retreat towards the west. After the rapid victorious attack, which lasted even less than the Soviet command had anticipated, during the early days of January, 1943, the ARMIR began its full retreat from the front along the Don. An extremely slow retreat, with very few vehicles, that the rapid Soviet troops decided to obstruct with a devious strategy that kept the Italian Royal Army troops in an unbearable state of constant alert. This consisted of circumventing and overtaking the long lines of Italian soldiers, then waiting to ambush them near villages or any precious shelter for the scattered soldiers, in need of some form of relief. Given the situation, paradoxically, it was precisely the Italian soldiers who, in order to continue their march west, attempted direct conflict with the enemy. This came to a head on January 26th, with the Battle of Nikolajewka, where, suffering enormous losses, the Italians managed to block the encircling manoeuvres and open themselves a gap towards the west. This occurred three days after the unconditional surrender of Stalingrad. After the Battle of Nikolajewka, the remaining ARMIR troops continued on foot for 600 kilometres to reach the collection camps for repatriation at the end of March. The thousands of soldiers captured by the Soviets during the retreat, were reduced to a very few who were lucky enough to return to Italy very sporadically after the end of the war. The desperate exhaustion of a defeated army in retreat, without vehicles or equipment, in sub-zero temperatures, exposed to enemy attacks and with few possibilities of survival is once more well-described by Rigoni-Stern: "...and as we walked, we dreamt of throwing ourselves into the snow: to sleep, to dream, and to vanish into nothingness, into oblivion, to then melt with the snow in spring vanishing into the humours of the earth".[112]

Between the 16th and 18th of December, during the very first days of the Soviet offensive, Captain Terragni suffered a tragic episode. The only evidence we have to reconstruct what happened during those days, is once more from Zuccoli, with whom evidently Terragni shared the events on his return to Italy. Not long before the unexpected attack, Captain Terragni, front line topographer, was sent on a mission to observe and identify certain enemy placements.[113] While he was performing his work, he was caught in the midst of harsh shellfire between a Soviet placement and an Italian post where he had taken shelter.

112. Mario Rigoni Stern, *Il sergente nella neve*, op. cit., p. 79. (Mario Rigoni Stern, *The Sergeant in the Snow*, NorthWestern University, 1998).

113. Luigi Zuccoli, "Terragni militare. La guerra. Mariuccia Casartelli. L'immatura scomparsa dell'amico e il mio 1943" in id., *Quindici anni di vita e di lavoro con l'amico e maestro architetto Giuseppe Terragni*, op. cit., p. 60.

It is not known whether he left to continue his work during a pause in the shellfire, or simply sudden panic during the violent attack, but he left the Italian post. Just a few moments later, the post was completely destroyed and all the occupants were killed. Very probably, Captain Terragni saw the scene and remained in shock. Luca Lanini wrote about the event: "this would explain the survivor syndrome Terragni suffered from on his return to Italy, and witnessed by Zuccoli, Sartoris and Giolli".[114] We have no information about what happened to Captain Terragni in the days between this episode and his reappearance among the Italian troops in retreat. We don't know what happened in the frozen steppe, whether he managed to return to his unit, or in the confusion, whether he joined up with another unit, or whether he remained alone, who knows where. The first news arrived a couple of weeks after the attack, when he was hospitalised in the Rykovo field hospital, a small town close to the front, notoriously famous for the cemetery of Italian troops.[115] He was almost immediately transferred to other hospitals in Stalino and in Voroscilovgrad. He was not physically wounded but was mentally deeply disturbed, although it is not known to what extent. The first written evidence was a brief letter that he wrote from one of the two hospitals to his brother Attilio: "After a few days of silence, I am sending you some news, which on the whole, is good. I am sick in hospital, but I hope to be better as soon as possible. Don't worry about me. I will send you news about my condition. My loving regards and heartfelt affection to you, and my dear nephews".[116] Other evidence is a draft letter he wrote at the same time, again from the army hospital, to a fellow soldier, a certain Colombini, asking him to intercede with the Command, to testify that he, Commander Terragni, had not abandoned his comrades, that he was not a deserter.[117] This is the first direct testimony of that "survivor syndrome" that was to torment Terragni for the rest of his life. In another draft letter, written to Colombini again, the same day, he was more specific about his state and where he was hospitalised: "Today I feel more relieved in body and spirit, and I wanted to write and thank you for all the truly affectionate help you gave me during those eventful days that were so painful because of my depressed state of health. At the moment, I am at the hospital in Stalino, after having spent time in the Rykovo field hospital. As I told you before, at the Voroscilovgrad hospital, my great worry was to make sure that my position was in order

114. Luca Lanini, "Commento" in Luigi Zuccoli, *Quindici anni di vita e di lavoro con l'amico e maestro architetto Giuseppe Terragni*, op. cit., p. 151.

115. Emilia Terragni, "Gli anni della guerra nel carteggio di Giuseppe Terragni, 1939-1943" in *Giuseppe Terragni. Opera completa*, op. cit., pp. 291-292.

116. Armed Forces post card from Terragni to his brother Attilio, January 2nd, 1943. Source: Terragni Archives.

117. "...to inform them of my inability to present myself at the Command on the day of my arrival in Voroscilovgrad because of the state of serious nervous shock in which I found myself [...] the directors of the hospital to whom I spoke, assured me that according to regulations, they would have informed my unit of my hospitalisation, but with the huge flow of patients in the hospital, I am afraid the procedure will take a long time [...]. So I have prepared two letters describing the situation, which I enclose". Armed Forces post card from Terragni to Colombini, January 4th, 1943. Source: Terragni Archives, personal correspondence, 1943, 8/6/39.

39

40

at the Artillery Command and our Army Corps Headquarters, and that they had been informed of my hospitalisation in Voroscilovgrad. I would appreciate it if you could ask again… Send me news of our companions that remained there, that we left behind… Send me news of Reggiani, the officers, our general, and all the officers we left at Ratchenskoi [sic], that day long ago in December".[118] A short time later, perhaps through intercession by his brother, or perhaps simply because of his condition, or perhaps because finally, the Italian Command realised that Captain Terragni had been in Russia for two years, an extremely rare event even for the Italian Army, he was repatriated with a red Cross train, one of the very rare trains that left the front for the west. So Terragni did not take part in the withdrawal of the Italian troops, and probably, the fact that he had not been part of the great collective catharsis, increased his sense of guilt even more, injuring his military pride even further. The long transfer by train took him to Cesenatico to the former Radaelli holiday camp, now transformed in military hospital. The medical report diagnosis was "serious symptomatic neuropsychiatric syndrome". Despite the seriousness of the medical report, he was one of the few to return alive from the Russian Campaign.

As soon as he arrived in Cesenatico on January 31st, therefore very rapidly, only a month after the Soviet offensive, he informed his brother Attilio of his return and reassured him about his state of health.[119] A few days later, Zuccoli went to visit him, and described the episode: "I remember that the wounded officer in the next bed warned me that given Terragni's psychic condition, he had taken away his revolver, to prevent any possibility of suicide. When I approached him, he saw me and shook my hand, then opening his eyes wide, he whispered: "Leave straight away! Don't stay anywhere near me, don't compromise yourself: I am a deserter, I will be shot!" You can imagine my shock and sorrow on hearing his words. However, little by little, after a few hours I managed to calm him only by trying to convince him that the situation was not so drastic. The news of the death of the members of the battalion he had just left had convinced him that he had fled from his battle station, and that therefore, he was a deserter, whereas he had simply and arduously returned to bring back the results of a mission accomplished".[120] On February 8th, Terragni wrote to the hospital director in a stentorian style, with several interruptions, asking him to deal with his fiancée, Mariuccia Casartelli, who had evidently also rushed to Cesenatico, and to convince

118. Armed Forces post card from Terragni to Colombini, January 4th, 1943. Source: Terragni Archives, personal correspondence.

119. Telegramme from Giuseppe Terragni to his brother Attilio. Source: Terragni Archives, personal correspondence.

120. Luigi Zuccoli, "Terragni militare. La guerra. Mariuccia Casartelli. L'immatura scomparsa dell'amico e il mio 1943" in id., *Quindici anni di vita e di lavoro con l'amico e maestro architetto Giuseppe Terragni*, op. cit., p. 61.

41

her to return to Como as soon as possible. At the bottom of the letter, in an unfinished sentence: "She doesn't know what I have to face… she is not at fault".[121] On the other hand, it was a well-known fact that Terragni did not appreciate the presence of his fiancée outside the routine of his life in Como. His great-nephew, Attilio Terragni, very plausibly imagines his uncle's convalescence like this: "The military camp in Cesenatico was an initial reception camp with large tents on the sand in a stark coastal landscape. The veterans lay on simple camp beds in these mobile structures. The light of the sea must have been an amazing surprise for Captain Terragni, when remembering the shining penetrating light of the Russian landscape. The light in Cesenatico, filtered by the tent fabric and the cracks through the canvas on the ground, was warm, welcoming, enveloping, even in a camp of temporary tents; with their curved mobile shapes they gently resisted the wind and the rain, bringing a certain atmosphere of home".[122]

This atmosphere of home probably increased his sense of guilt even more: the guilt of having survived. After about three weeks, he was discharged, and two days later, his brother Attilio left Como by car with a driver to finally bring him home. The patient's release took place without any trouble. Giuseppe seemed resigned, sometimes absent. After dealing with the formalities, they collected Giuseppe's few belongings (a large part had remained in Russia, including drawings, photos and short films) and completed the procedure that put an end to more than three years of army life, two of which spent at war. Because of the daily allied bombing, Attilio and the driver decided to leave that evening and late that night the car with the three men arrived in Como in via Indipendenza 23. It drove through the gate and parked in the small courtyard overlooked by the family home and the studio. Giuseppe had been calm during the trip home, but as soon as he got out of the car he began to shout at the top of his voice, kicking the car, and manhandling anybody who came near him.

To immobilise Giuseppe, 6 foot 2 inches tall, in a fit of rage, it took three people: his two brothers Attilio and Alberto, and the driver. They managed to control him and force him back into the car. They took him to Olgiate Comasco, not far from Como, to the villa where Alberto lived with his wife. We do not have information on his stay there, but considering what happened later, it is to be concluded that Giuseppe's condition did not improve. His brothers decided to entrust Giuseppe to the care of Professor Ugo Cerletti, the inventor of the new electroshock therapy.

121. Letter to the Director of the Cesenatico Hospital, February 8th, 1943 (AGT 967).

122. Attilio Terragni, "Una vecchia storia" in Valerio Paolo Mosco, L'ultima cattedrale, Sagep edizioni, Genoa, p. 12.

42

Captain Terragni was admitted to Cerletti's clinic in Pavia on March 5th, 1943, where he began a series of eight or nine sessions that finished at the beginning of July, only a few days before his death.[123] Mario Radice described this period: "When Terragni returned to Italy he was completely changed: he had seen and experienced horrific situations… and he had been convinced of a victory, he thought they could win this war… even in normal times, Terragni sometimes had strange reactions, so you can imagine his condition after his return from Russia. His friends were shocked to see him so distressed… I knew him very well, so I did not find him particularly changed… but even his brother Attilio was disturbed to see him in this condition. Attilio had been in Rhodes during the war and had met the inventor of electroshock therapy, Professor Cerletti from Pavia, who subjected Giuseppe to eight or nine sessions of very intense treatment, and every time, he lost consciousness".[124] Certain family rumours insist that it was not his older brother who suggested the treatment, but Piero Lingeri who was well-introduced into Milanese society and probably knew Cerletti and his therapy. As was previously described, relations between Lingeri and Terragni had been deteriorating for some time and when Terragni left for the army, the question of the division of the commissions still remained dramatically unresolved, as did the assignment for the Brera Academy commission. Lingeri was in the centre of the conflict that existed between Terragni, and Figini and Pollini. Therefore, at least in theory, for Lingeri, Terragni was an inconvenience, and putting him out of the picture would have been a relief for an architect who was not especially talented, but who was very attached to his career. Conjectures of this kind without proof could hint at some form of interference in Terragni's death by Lingeri, similar to the theory that Salieri might have been involved in the death of an already debilitated Mozart. The fact remains that partly because of his determination, that often slid into a certain arrogance, Terragni had become rather irritating for many in the somewhat lethargic Como. He had been that way since the time of the Novocomum episode and the town planning scheme, and his annoying behaviour had reached its peak with the issues concerning the Cortesella project and Casa Vietti. The ruins were still an unresolved problem when he returned, and were obstructing a speculation project that involved certain powerful entrepreneurs in Como who were very interested in the project and intended to relaunch it when the war was over.

123. The first electroshock session occurred on March 8th, 1943, and the last on July 4th, 1943. Source: Luca Lanini, "Commento" in Luigi Zuccoli, *Quindici anni di vita e lavoro con l'amico e maestro architetto Giuseppe Terragni*, op. cit., pp. 152-153.

124. Angelo Maugeri,"Intervista a Maugeri" in *Mario Radice*, R. Cantiani, Como, 1986, p. 28. Terragni was admitted to Professor Cerletti's clinic in Pavia, and received a post card from their studio engineer, Renato Uslenghi: "I am constantly kept informed of your progress and I would come to visit you, but I am afraid of disturbing your peace and quiet. I receive your news from your brothers and Mrs Zuccoli, but, I am a true doubting Thomas, and I will not be satisfied until I have seen for myself that you are still the same old Peppino. I have nothing new to tell you that you don't already know. Como is the same Como you left behind you: Instead, I will come and take a look at Pavia, that you probably know as well as I do… not much. Keep healthy, eat and drink well: When a machine is properly oiled, it runs well. Keep well and I will see you soon. A warm embrace, Uslenghi". Source: Terragni Archives, personal correspondence.

He was also an irritation in Milan, evident in the very poor relations he had with Figini and Pollini, and in Rome, where many people were afraid that one of his probable commissions would succeed, and could threaten the consolidated network for sharing out commissions that had been well established for some time. Apart from all these aspects, it seems very surprising how, in a milieu like that of the Terragni family, well educated and experienced, and of the people close to them, that they did not consider the fact, which was quite well-known at the time, that electroshock was a dangerous treatment, and not to be used lightly, as it was often fatal for patients with a family history of strokes, like the Terragni family. Giuseppe's mother had died of a stroke when he was little more than an adolescent. However, it must also be said that in the spring of 1943, after the defeats in El Alamein and Russia, plus the ever-increasing allied bombings, the situation in Italy had evolved from difficult to dramatic, and in this scenario, any decisions, not only political and military, but also personal, were often made hastily, and even rashly. In fact, after 1943, the war had changed from being exclusively a public matter to a private concern that was just as dramatic. Despite the intensity and frequency of the electroshock treatment, it did not seem to bring Terragni any relief; on the contrary he was even more depressed.[125] A photo of him during that period shows him in impeccable army uniform, in front of a photo of some authority, perhaps the king. Terragni is still wearing the beard he grew in Russia and seems to have lost weight. His shoulders are not as powerful as before, he has a glazed expression, and is looking upwards towards some obscure other place. The photo seems to embody the words used by Alberto Sartoris in describing the last period of his friend's life: "We had always known him so strong and dynamic, powerfully undefeated, and he returned among us for a few days, dejected, spiritualised, dehumanised, almost sanctified by his sufferings".[126] The man everybody knew so well was unrecognisable. Bardi went to see him and was shocked: "I went early in the morning. I ran to his house and he was coming down the stairs. His smile was different, it was very faint. He started to talk about what would happen in Italy. We all knew it was the end, but Terragni was convinced that the situation would develop. I tried to change the subject, but he would not listen. We went out and he wanted to take me to the house where Sant'Elia's sister lived. We sat on a low wall: he would not change the subject, he could not come to terms with the fact that Italy could not win.

125. One of Terragni's last professional communications was a letter written on May 19th, 1943, from the Study and Information Centre for glass application in construction and internal furnishing. The Study Centre invited Terragni to deal with construction problems after the war, "asking if he considered Wright's research appropriate". Source: Terragni Archives, personal correspondence.

126. Alberto Sartoris, *Presenza di Giuseppe Terragni* in *Prima mostra commemorativa di Giuseppe Terragni*, exhibition catalogue, op. cit.

Architecture had dropped into second place. He told me how much he was suffering because he was not fighting. He described episodes from the Russian Campaign as many as three times over… we spent the day together, and that was the last time I saw him".[127] The architectural critic, Raffaello Giolli, who joined the Resistance shortly after, and who was to lose his life like his son, wrote: "We met him during that time, he was nothing like the old Terragni: he seemed to be overwhelmed by a persecution complex. He would leave the house intentionally to go and see some friend and ask his forgiveness for having said something – who knows what or when. It was on one of those days that he went to see his fiancée, and climbing the stairs, his heart gave out".[128] Similar comments were made by Guido Frette: "I went to visit Terragni in Como in 1943. We spent almost the whole afternoon inside the church of San Fedele; he explained his ideas, perhaps his dreams, about bringing the church back to its original state. At first he seemed the same person, despite the mental breakdown he had suffered after the retreat from Russia; but looking at him more closely, you could see the sadness in his expression that he was not able to hide … as if everything inside him had collapsed".[129] Giorgio Ciucci interpreted these descriptions in this way: "I then wondered whether the final mental collapse, the depression that overwhelmed him, was caused by the awareness of what Fascism had actually represented, something in which he had deeply believed; it might have explained the collapse of the productive force between his personal expressive emotions and his commitment to the public, between being an artist and the social utility of his role. So, on the contrary, not in relation to Fascism, but a rupture with his own existence within Fascism".[130] An interpretation that does not take into consideration another fundamental aspect of Terragni's personality, his deeply Christian beliefs, an aspect that seemed to prevail after his return from Russia. Mario Radice, who spent a lot of time with him after his return from Russia also spoke about Terragni's spiritualization, about a man who, perhaps for the first time, in surrendering himself to his Christian faith, discovered "the incomparable greatness of humility".[131]

There are some artistic traces of the difficult period in which Terragni was undergoing electroshock treatment in the clinic in Pavia, initially hospitalised, then going back and forward from Como: a painting and some sketches of a city rich in the Romanesque architecture he had always loved so much.

127. Quoted in L'Architettura. Cronache e storia, XV, n. 163, May 1969, p. 273.

128. Raffaello Giolli, "Mondiano-Terragni-Cattaneo" in Costruzioni-Casabella, 191-192, Nov-Dec 1943, quoted from Giorgio Ciucci, "Terragni e l'Architettura" in Giuseppe Terragni. Opera completa, op. cit., p. 70.

129. Cited in L'architettura. Cronache e storia, op. cit., p. 273.

130. Giorgio Ciucci, "Terragni e l'Architettura" in Giuseppe Terragni. Opera completa, op. cit. p. 25.

131. Mario Radice, Ritratto di Giuseppe Terragni, in Prima mostra commemorativa di Giuseppe Terragni, exhibition catalogue, op. cit.

43

The little painting is quite a common landscape, lopsided, and painted with a technique that was not at all up to Terragni's normal standards. As often occurred with his paintings, it is mounted in a large original frame that almost reduces the subject to a rough sketch in various earth colours. The brush-strokes, partly executed with a palette-knife, are thick and dense, like his other paintings, especially his landscapes, and recall the expressionism of Nolde and the disturbed despair of Van Gogh. More interesting are his sketches: drawn in pencil with his usual fine, slightly quivering, almost vanishing lines, they demonstrate a Terragni who seemed to have retained his liveliness and freshness.

One of the drawings is unusual. It is a sketch of what seems to be the waiting room of the doctor who was treating him, Dr. Guido Gastaldi. Terragni, who had drawn on the doctor's letter-headed paper, probably pilfered from the reception desk, portrayed the entrance of the surgery from the interior. It is composed of what would be called today a "wall unit", including the door, a coat rack, and cupboards. Here was an unexpected record of modern architecture that Terragni analysed, even measuring the height of the mobile drawer unit: 40 cm. Captain Terragni, topographer, back from the war, noticed an unexpected fragment of modern architecture, a piece that Pagano would have called "current", and evidently, he thought about the concept. The other three drawings are views of historic areas in Pavia where unexpectedly, he seized the vernacular aspect: that almost endless overlaying of marks, memories, and fragments typical of Medieval Lombardy towns. In these sketches (in which a couple feature San Teodoro, a Lombardic church that Terragni mistakenly identified, writing the name of Santa Teodolinda) there is the same inadvertent, accidental, slightly quirky effect of some of his photos from Yugoslavia and Russia. Observing these sketches, it is surprising to note that Terragni, who had always been immersed in the paradisiac order of his abstract architecture, paused to reflect on something that has no order and will never have any: that mysterious harmony which is created with spontaneous architecture, developed without architects. In fact, it was the first time he sketched vernacular architecture, evidently in search of new creative possibilities.

If Terragni, the man, returned "spiritualised" from the war, Terragni the artist already showed these signs before his departure. In the late 1930s, he was strongly influenced by a strange, theatrical, talkative personage, well-cultured, resolute and distracted, like many other Italian intellectuals of the period: Franco Ciliberti. Ciliberti had the habit of travelling back and forward between Milan and Como holding brief engaging conferences dedicated to what he considered to be the essential values for western culture; supratemporal values which mankind needed to re-embrace.[132] Ciliberti, who saw himself as an Italian Spengler, believed that historical periods were defined because they assumed form thanks to the work of those he emphatically called "creators", authentic geniuses, practically magicians, able to give life to what Ciliberti himself defined as "primordial values". A concept of those ethereal, fascinating, primordial values similar to the timeless archetypes that nourish the human spirit. He felt that man's destiny was linked with primordial values, which over time, tend to fade and disappear; therefore, the role of the "creators" was to regenerate these values. The point was that, although archetypal, primordial values had no specific form, but rather assumed a form each time, according to the period and the artistic complexion of the individual creator: they were embodied in the work of the creator. So the same primordial values could refer to a Romanesque cathedral, an architectural project by Michelangelo, and a fragment of a vernacular Medieval building; a captivating concept although perhaps not very clear. Terragni was fascinated by these theories and with Ciliberti, he founded a magazine *Valori primordiali*, in which he was responsible for the graphics and elegant layout. Spending time with Ciliberti, Terragni felt himself increasingly more a "creator", a conviction that led him to consider architecture as a mystical activity, that, in its sublime form, transcended styles and periods.[133] Terragni, the "modern" artist, assumed the task of giving life to primordial values through abstraction. He considered this task as a mission, because he felt that abstraction was precisely the best means to grasp the indefinable "primordiality" he was seeking. In fact, abstraction had the potential to gather the essential elements of a figure, transferring them to the sphere of ideas. In other words, in transfiguration, abstraction finds its fulfilment.[134] It was by no means coincidental that the subject of transfiguration (an extremely Christian theme) often appeared in Ciliberti's conferences, and was evoked explicitly in the Manifesto of Primordial Values that Terragni helped to write with the others.[135] In this vast program converged the dream of Nietzsche's 'greatness', memories of the mystical numbers

132. The magazine, *Valori primordiali*, appeared in Como in 1938. The director was Franco Ciliberti, the editorial staff included Soldati, Ghiringhelli, Reggiani, Rho, Licini, Terragni, Radice, Cattaneo, Lingeri, and Badiali. Only one issue was published. Recommended writings by Franco Ciliberti: *Storia degli ideali*, edited by Elena Di Raddo, Cattaneo edizioni Archives, Como, 2003.

133. The idea of supratemporality was a constant concept in a large part of Italian culture at that time. One has only to remember the radical idealism of Giovanni Gentile. In 1922, a fundamental artistic figure for successive development, Gino Severini, wrote: "There is not one period that interests us in particular more than another, we are interested in the invariant constant of every period: not the styles, but what internally organises the style, the initial cause that produces the result [...]. I would like artists to be enlightened, initiated individuals, like the followers of Pythagoras, seeking the scientific notions necessary to understand the universe, not according to its appearance, but to its constructive laws". Gino Severini, *Du cubisme au classicisme*, Povolozky editore, Paris, 1922. Quoted in Armando Dal Fabbro, *Il progetto razionalista. Indagine sulle procedure compositive delle grandi architetture di Terragni*, Mucchi editore, Modena, 1993, pp. 31-33. (Gino Severini, *From Cubism to Classicism*, Francis Boutle Publishers, 2001).

134. In deeply profound writings, Giorgio Ciucci seized on significant aspects of Terragni's research in the last period of his career, which Ciucci defined as "absolute form", placing it in relation with the classical impetus of the ultimate Terragni: "Classicism is not simply a comparison with the classical object, and least of all, its literal response, but rarefaction of the intrinsic laws of architecture [...] the architecture of Terragni supposes an order already established, he does not invoke it, but evokes it". Giorgio Ciucci, *Gli architetti ed il fascismo*, Giulio Einaudi editore, Turin, 1989, p. 147.

135. The Manifesto of *Valori primordiali* appeared in 1941, signed by F. Ciliberti, G. Terragni, P. Lingeri, C. Badiali, M. Rho, O. Licini, B. Munari, M. Nizzoli, M. Radice, A. Soldati. Antonino Saggio wrote: "primary force", but understood, not in the mystical sense but totally figuratively. Antonino Saggio, *Giuseppe Terragni 1904/1943*, Laterza edizioni, Bari, 1995, p. 15. A fundamental text for understanding the context, halfway between the modern and the mystical in those years, is a text that was essential for the abstract and primordial artists who gravitated around Milan and Como at that time: Carlo Belli, *Kn*, All'insegna del pesce d'oro edizioni, Milan, 1972 (first edition 1935).

136. "It is commonly said that the point of departure of Romanesque architecture is to be sought in the work of the 'Comancine Masters', a guild that was based in Lombardy, and perhaps near Como from where the term 'Comacine is thought to originate, although others believe the name was derived from their construction methods 'cum machinis'. However, it is not possible to state that these masters created a new architectural language that was independent from tradition: on the contrary, many traditional Byzantine styles and influences from Ravenna can be found in their work", Giulio Carlo Argan, *L'architettura protocristiana, preromanica, e romanica*, Novissima enciclopedia monografica illustrata, Florence, 1937, pp. 16-17.

137. Alberto Sartoris, *La lunga marcia dell'arte astratta in Italia*, Vanni Scheiwiller editore, Milan, 1980, p. 88.

138. Franco Ciliberti, *Storia degli ideali*, op. cit, p. 121.

139. Reccommended reading for details on Terragni's spirituality and the sphere to which it refers: Alberto Cuomo, *Terragni ultimo*, Guida edizioni, Naples, 1988.

140. Explicity dedicated to this project is the book by Valerio Paolo Mosco, *L'ultima cattedrale*, Sagep, Genoa, 2005.

of Pythagoras, Platonism, and Neoplatonism (very familiar to Terragni) and lessons from great Christian mystics. There is an anecdote that helps understand the spirit that hovered among some of the eccentric members of Terragni's circle at that time. During the war, Cesare Cattaneo, who could be considered Terragni's disciple, had speculated on the idea, when the war was over, of setting up a hermitage in the Alps for Christian abstract artists: as leader of the hermitage, he proposed the most talented and determined among them, Giuseppe Terragni. There is another element that helps understand not simply the poetic but also the temperament of Terragni. As well as considering himself a "creator", he also felt he was a Comacine Master, in other words, one of the legendary Medieval guild of stonemasons who built the Romanesque cathedrals. Originally from northern Lombardy and Switzerland they travelled around Europe, taking with them their initiatic building techniques, where craftsmanship and faith were bonded in an inseparable spirit.[136] Terragni had felt his Comacine Master nature right from the time when he would go to the Casa del Fascio worksite at dawn and destroy any marble slabs that were not perfectly pristine to prevent them from being used in construction, or when, like Michelangelo, he would go to the quarries to choose the best quality marble.[137] His inflexibility, his persistence, to the point of clashing with anybody who might obstruct him in his work, his obsessive behaviour that amazed his friends, should all be seen in the childish and brash personification of a Comacine Master able to embody primordial values in abstract form. After all, it was Ciliberti himself who wrote: "architectural forms are not something external, but allow the original essence of life to filter through, and in doing so, save the world from the mediocrity that generally exists".[138] After his return from the vast hurricane (this is how Terragni defined the war in Russia) he no longer asked primordial values to save the world from mediocrity, but to save his personal spiritual and artistic life, and by extension, the life of an era. All this explains his last project, the cathedral.[139]

The cathedral project is composed of a series of architectural objects placed in sequence.[140] The first is what seems to be the horizontal body of a structure suspended above the ground, but that could also be interpreted as a large screen. It is composed of a frame inside which are several compartments that enclose large decorative panels,

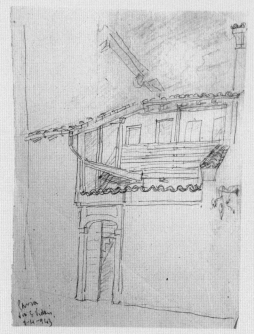

44

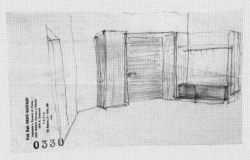

45

probably in high relief, similar to those that Terragni thought of commissioning from Mario Sironi for the Danteum. The large frame is the same length as the entire facade, and resembles an actual iconostasis, but, instead of being placed in front of the sanctuary, it is positioned outside the church: there is a significant symbolic intent that could be understood as an outward-reaching proclamatory choice to express a message that can be transmitted to all. An interesting element is the vertical slit in the centre of the frame: a deep slit, almost like a crevice, piercing the whole length of the nave, perhaps designed to reveal the tabernacle to the exterior. Above the decorative panels, the frame continues towards the sky, rising upwards, as if supported by two slightly diverging masts linked by a catenary chain that recalls a Baroque festoon. On the aerial frame there are some rapid sketches similar to the angels that Lucio Fontana drew during the same period. Behind this element is the actual cathedral that appears like a cave which is entered through a low, gently stretched arch. The interior of the large cave, which can be imagined from the rapid sketches of the floor plan that have remained, is sealed by a curved hyperbole that funnels towards an apse, decorated in a manner similar to the iconostasis at the entrance. Therefore, the internal space is formed by the joining of two figures: the stretched low arch at the entrance, and the vertical arch of the apse. The resulting geometry has a clear religious significance: it is the abstract representation of the route followed by the faithful from their human dimension (horizontal) to reach their divine nature (vertical). The cathedral is supported on a classical continuous plinth base raised from the ground by a few low steps; a delicate gesture of separation necessary to disengage itself from the earth. The dimensions are striking. They can be calculated thanks to the small figures that Terragni sketched next to the building. Vast dimensions, unusual for Terragni until that moment, except for the Cortesella project; he had always expressed himself through controllable size, like that of Como. A dimensional leap which reveals an attraction for the vast scale, demonstrated for the first time in his photos of the Russian steppe, which pay tribute to the immense, absolute, spiritualised space, without comparison. The sketch of the floor plan presents another hint concerning spiritualisation. The sketch shows the apse hyperbole is interrupted by two slits, one on each side, at the height of the transept: two slots of vertical light that would probably have continued for the entire height of the structure.

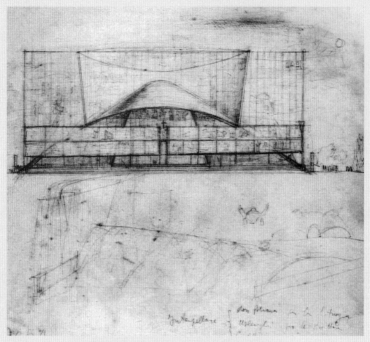

46

47

After these slots, continuing towards the apse, is another, more open hyperbole, with a wider flare than the first. The double slots of light would have created a transversal illumination at the height of the transept,which would have attenuated the chthonic atmosphere of the interior, dissolving the apse and making the high relief decorations at the end of the church visible, thanks to the "Bernini" side lighting effect. But this was not the only role of the two light slots. In his sketch, with a strong mark that does not refer to any architectural element, Terragni underlined the dimension of the apse and the transept. These two marks form a Latin Cross, the epitome of Christian symbolism, that Terragni with mystical reticence, evoked in absentia, as if the cross was composed of a void.

All the elements of Terragni's architecture are summarised in his cathedral. He had already designed a large parabolic cave in a project in the early 1930s, also for a cathedral; the slightly raised plinth base was included in all the public projects of his last period; the suspended frame was part of the project for the Milan Trade Fair; the central slot was featured in the first project for Palazzo Littorio, and the series of decorative panels is similar to those designed for the Danteum. Therefore, we find Terragni the mannerist, or rather, mannerist of himself, as with most mature artists who have consolidated their expressive language while awaiting something that will transcend it. But, despite the fact that the component elements were already familiar, in his last project they were assembled in a previously unseen combination, not at all achieved through the rationale of abstract composition. They were assembled to evoke a figure, and this was the innovative aspect. This theory is corroborated by the fact that the artist presented the whole concept in a way that, for him, was totally unusual: seen from the front, as if the viewer was facing a Byzantine devotional icon. In fact, Terragni created an abstract transfiguration of a Medieval painting, famous in Lombardy and the Veneto region, whose popular devotion has resisted over time: the Virgin of Mercy. This iconic example became particularly famous because of the painting by Piero della Francesca, which, like many of the high-reliefs to be found in Venetian streets, features the imposing figure of the Virgin in the centre, hieratically facing the viewer, and protectively gathering under her mantle the vulnerable faithful who kneel before her seeking mercy and forgiveness.

48

141. "And yet, some hope still remained: in his declarations one can read the frustration of the convalescent, recalling the Magic Mountain, the painful convalescence of one who has had to face the most tragic of illnesses, seeing the collapse of his beliefs before his own eyes. But his other belief still remained, and there is perhaps a strong reason behind the fact that Terragni's last creation was a project for a cathedral; here too a church in which abstraction holds back in the face of the desire to preserve, to safeguard a symbolic criterion, to propose an image that is able, in some way, to be representative. In this case, perhaps, when designing his stretched arch, Terragni was thinking of the same iconology of Milan Cathedral, alluding to its Medieval facade, inspired by the mantle of the Virgin, open in symbolic Majesty". Paolo Portoghesi, *I grandi architetti del Novecento*, Newton & Compton editore, 2013, p. 354. Also see: Paolo Portoghesi, "La fede in Terragni", in *Giuseppe Terragni. Materiali per comprendere Terragni ed il suo tempo*, edited by Alberto Artioli and Giancarlo Borellini vol.II, Betagamma editore, Viterbo, 1996, p. 27. Also recommended in the same book, the contribution by Marco Dezzi Bardeschi, "La conversione di Terragni", pp. 17-22.

142. There is an interesting comment on this subject by Cesare Cattaneo: "Here, times are getting harder and discoveries become more clear in each one of us (the young analyse things more deeply) the Catholic aspect of our civilisation... the most recent social experiences have confirmed how useless and bloody this is, to do it all over again, rejecting the religious aspect", Ornella Selvafolta, "I percorsi di un giovane architetto", in id., *Prefigurazioni plastiche. Cesare Cattaneo architetto*, Studio Logos, Como, 1989, p. 32.

143. Umberto Boccioni, "La grande madre. Pensieri sull'arte", in *I quaderni di via del vento*, n. 72, Pistoia, 2014, p. 22. Quoted in Valerio Paolo Mosco, "Astrattismo lirico sub specie lucis" in Luigi Zuccoli, *Quindici anni di vita e di lavoro con l'amico e maestro architetto Giuseppe Terragni*, op. cit., p. LXXXIII-C.

Mercy and forgiveness: this is what Captain Terragni sought on his return from Russia. In exchange, he gave proof of a devotion that was explicitly featured in his work for the first time. Terragni's project for a cathedral is the only modern example of devotional and symbolic architecture, not only of a creed, but also of an existential condition. It was a rift in comparison to the secular and basically materialistic orthodoxy of Modernism. Through that spiritualism fostered during the war, the result of the pain he experienced, Terragni opened up towards a new form of expression: not so much in the form itself (Terragni adopted his well-established elements) but in the content. Let us compare the photomontage with the cathedral of Cremona alongside the Giuliani-Frigerio building, and the dyad of the Virgin of Mercy next to Terragni's cathedral. In both cases the relationship between the two figures is based on the analogy, but if, in the first case, the analogy is compositional, given the similar rhythm and score, in the second case, the analogy is no longer compositional, but concerns the figure in its entirety: it is an analogy created from the transfiguration of a figure. Paolo Portoghesi is correct when he sees constant tension between figuration and abstraction, in the continued intertwining between these two extremes, considered as incompatible and contradictory in Modernism; this does not apply only in the more intimate nature of Terragni's architecture, but also the fundamental theme of the great iconological and iconographic tradition Terragni intended to take inspiration from.[141] And it is here that the "masks" described by Tafuri are removed to reveal a face: the face of a Christian artist.[142] The hypothesis of an art form able to go beyond the dichotomy between figuration and abstraction was proposed decades before by another Italian artist, Umberto Boccioni, this time not with a Christian motivation, but simply to express a dynamic, liberating spirituality worthy of an era, able to exceed itself, as sought by Nietzsche.

In his anguished diaries, Boccioni wrote about his aspiration to express through his art "the spiritual sensation of objects" and had called this desire "physical transcendentalism". In his intention, it was something to be achieved with a form of painting and sculpture, that could exist beyond the contraposition between figuration and abstraction.[143] When considering Terragni's cathedral, we can use the term physical transcendentalism: it is a project based on rarefication (precisely in order to become transfigured, every element of the composition is taken to the maximum of physical rarefication) in order to obtain a diffused sensation of intangible merciful grace. Therefore, with the cathedral, he laid the foundations for a new language: an abstract and figurative language, and a spiritual and transfigurative language at the same time. A language of which only the traces remain since Terragni died just a few days after designing the facade of his cathedral. But this project does not appear to show any regrets: it seems to represent the summary of his life. A sentence by Virginia Woolf on the capacity of writing to create transfiguration of life could be written underneath the sketch of the cathedral. Woolf wrote: "This endless order opens up around us. The discontinuity of light and darkness is transformed into a luminous halo, in a semi-transparent shell that surrounds our being completely and in this way, embraces our existence from beginning to end".[144]

We have no information on whether Terragni's cathedral was commissioned or not. It seems strange that a man as pragmatic as Terragni would have become involved in a project without a commission. It is also strange that for a project of this importance and size, there is no correspondence with a potential client. One, albeit remote, possibility could be linked with the mysterious commission he was sent during the first year he spent in Russia, which had excited him for the somewhat Futuristic idea of a collaboration with Como, thousands of miles away, in the midst of a war. To add to the mystery, there are a few lines written by Terragni at the bottom of the page to remind himself to consult a priest for advice on liturgical organisation, an engineer for the ambitious structure, and two artists to create the decorative panels. This reminder could corroborate the theory that the project was a concrete commission. Another theory is that although the project might have begun with a precise commission, with his return to Italy, in a condition that had changed completely, this project became a personal experience. Another mystery is the disappearance of the other plans and drawings. Given the considerable level of detail in the facade, it is plausible that there were other plans, cross-sections, and perhaps even perspectives or axonometric projections. If it refers to a commission that was sent to him in Russia, it is possible that the remaining sketches and plans were lost there, or were lost in Como.[145] Another theory is that the project was represented by Terragni as a unique sacred apparition, as an architectural annunciation, and for that reason he designed only

144. Virginia Woolf, *Spegnere le luci e guardare di tanto in tanto il mondo. Riflessioni sulla scrittura*, edited by Federico Sabatini, Minimum fax, Rome, 2017.

145. Ada F. Marcianò quotes the following words, although she does not provide the source: "During the endless winter days in the shelters… he worked intensely on a project that was enormously important to him: the project of a truly modern cathedral. When he came back from the front, his fate already forecast, he excitedly told a friend that he had finally found the solution. Unfortunately, most of the drawings remained in Russia and were lost in the final disaster", *Giuseppe Terragni. Opera completa 1925-1943*, op. cit., p. 280.

a single facade, drawing plans that were little defined, or defined only for a single presentation. The fact remains that the few sketches that survived have always placed historians and critics in an awkward position. Zevi almost turned a blind eye to this project that did not fit his theories, using it surreptitiously as a pretext to describe the mental decline of its designer, by now conscious of his political errors, nothing more.[146] Ada F. Marcianò's superficial and hasty opinion, considered the facade "symmetrical and static", attributing the design to Terragni's mental confusion.[147] It took many years before critics re-evaluated the cathedral, granting it fair recognition. Among the first was Thomas L. Schumacher, who appropriately wrote: "As happens with many talented artists, their final works form a kind of prelude to something that is then never achieved".[148] It was Daniel Libeskind who unexpectedly understood the spiritual force of the cathedral. He wrote: "Terragni's last fantastic design for a cathedral is his response to faith. After all the closures, all the suffering, after the destruction of cities, destruction of his friends, destruction of his country, destruction of Europe, destruction of the world, Terragni came to see something else; he managed to see something like an apparition, which, like a veil, inserts itself into the pure geometry of previous eras and bends them to create new scenarios. The cathedral design is both sombre and symmetrical, but it contains a new constellation of forces within it. These are no longer simple geometries, but signs of Terragni's extraordinary spiritual development; it is immediately evident that what he went through influenced his life and his future work. If we make a very large blow up of the cathedral drawing, we can see an extraordinary tiny figure on the left. This is probably the last sketch that Terragni ever drew: a human being with outstretched arms. What does it represent? It shows the vulnerability of human life, of the human being in itself, its hands open, the hope for the future and the fact that history is not over, and that we will always be under (some form of) pressure, that there will always be wars, conflicts, financial problems, and in this, we must not waver from the path of righteousness, allowing ourselves to be tempted by perversion, but follow the path of life that is open and free".[149] Perhaps it also suggests something else: that it is pain that forges creativity, making works necessary for their own sake, and that pain, overcome and transfigured, but never erased, produces the joy described by Nietzsche in his Zarathustra:

146. Bruno Zevi, L'Architettura. Cronache e storia, op. cit., pp. 272-273.

147. Ada F. Marcianò, Giuseppe Terragni. Opera completa 1925-1943, op. cit., p. 280.

148. Thomas L. Schumacher, G. Terragni 1904-1943, Electa edizioni, Milan, 1992, p. 277.

149. Daniel Libeskind, "Life after life", text from a conference held in Como on April 18th, 2004, in Attilio Terragni, Daniel Libeskind, Paolo Rosselli, Atlante Terragni, Skira, Milan, 2004, pp. 59-60.

the indescribable joy of rebirth, and in this specific case, rebirth in the faith.

It was July, Captain Giuseppe Terragni had been back in Italy for six months. It was hot, and despite the war, his brother Attilio decided to take his children of whom Giuseppe was very fond, away from hot and humid Como for a vacation, leaving Giuseppe alone in the house in via Indipendenza. Evidently his condition was not especially worrying, and in Como, only a short distance away, were his fiancée Mariuccia and his friends at the bar Polonio. On the morning of July 12th, 1943, one of his close friends from the bar, Augusto De Benedetti, personally related that he had invited him to eat at the Becco Giallo restaurant. They walked together towards the home of Terragni's fiancée in Piazza Mazzini. De Benedetti said that they parted company at the door, only a few moments before the tragedy.[150] However, De Benedetti's version did not coincide with that of another friend, the painter Radice, who described the following: "He was at home alone and was preparing his lunch, he felt ill and had phoned his fiancée to warn her and left the house to go to her home three hundred metres away, leaving all the lights on, a saucepan on the gas flame, and all the doors wide open. His fiancée who was waiting for him on the balcony, saw him arriving, and went immediately to meet him in the stairs and saw him fall and hit his head. Terragni fell on the first floor landing and died… the doctor who rushed to the house certified that Terragni had a bruise in the cerebellum area, caused by clotted blood. Probably a brain haemorrhage, but it was never able to be established if it was caused by the blow that occurred during his fall".[151] Alberto Longatti described: "In a pocket of his threadbare military greatcoat that he continued to wear in the house, there was a small bunch of dried wild flowers gathered in the steppes of the Don".[152] After his death, certain people like Gardella, and indirectly Zevi, spread the theory of a suicide, describing a Tarragni who was so disturbed that he threw himself into the stairwell in his fiancée's house and that, to prevent a scandal, the family hushed up the story. Bardi's theory is more probable: "I don't know how Terragni died. I always thought and felt that he could have died from suffering and anguish".[153] The fact remains that a figure so strongly linked with his own era died at thirty-nine years of age, on the day Rome was bombed, and five days before the hearing of the Grand

150. Bruno Zevi, *L'architettura. Cronache e storia*, op. cit., p. 273.

151. A. Maugeri, "Interview with Maugeri", in *Mario Radice*, op. cit., p. 28, quoted by Luca Lanini, "Commento", in Luigi Zuccoli, *Quindici anni di vita e lavoro con l'amico e maestro architetto Giuseppe Terragni*, op. cit., p. 152

152. Bruno Zevi, *L'Architettura. Cronache e storia*, op. cit., p. 273.

153. Ibidem.

Council that, following the military disaster and persistent bombing of Italian cities, passed a vote of no confidence in Mussolini, forcing him to resign. Shortly after, civil war broke out in Italy. The funeral of the architect, Giuseppe Terragni, a well-known figure in Como, member of a well-known family, was held a few days later in grand style, as can be seen in various photographs. Among those from Milan who were present, were the architect Muzio, and Portaluppi who had been his professor at Politecnico University in Milan.

The photos of the funeral procession following the coffin from his home in via Indipendenza to the church, with a crowd of Black Shirts and Roman Salutes, seem to bid farewell not only to Captain Terragni but to the world they represent.

Not long after the ceremony, Luigi Zuccoli, exhausted and dazed after the disappearance of his *maestro*, described an episode that happened to him: "I was on leave during the early days of August 1943 because of my father's death that had occurred on the 6th; I had heard that Cesare Cattaneo was hospitalised at Santa Anna and went to visit him.

The incident is still deeply impressed in my memory. He was sitting on his bed, very pale and white with an ice pack on his head. As soon as he saw me, he opened his eyes wide and said: 'You saw Peppino, he just left my room'. Terragni had been dead since July 19th! I said Terragni had probably gone down the stairs, but that I had taken the elevator and I had not seen him".[154] A few days later, on August 24th, 1943, Cattaneo died of tuberculosis at the age of thirty-one. With the successive death of Franco Ciliberti, all the leading figures of the Lyrical Abstraction movement in Como disappeared in perfect conjunction with the end of an era. Simone Weil wrote these words: "When pain and weariness reach the point of causing a sense of perpetuity to be born in the soul, through contemplating this perpetuity with acceptance and love, we are snatched away into eternity".[155] It is possible that the sense of the end of Captain Terragni is contained in these words.

154. Luca Lanini, "Commento" in Luigi Zuccoli, *Quindici anni di vita e di lavoro con l'amico e maestro architetto Giuseppe Terragni*, op. cit., pp. 75-76.

155. Simone Weil, *L'ombra e la grazia*, Bompiani, Milano, 2011, p. 41 (Simone Weil, *Gravity and Grace*. Routledge & Kegan Paul, 1952).

"[...] as the intensity of the spiritual
gaze and the visual penetration
of man gradually increases, the greater
the distance or space around him
appears, the deeper his world
becomes, and greater the number
of new stars on the horizon,
new images, new enigmas..."

Massimo Bontempelli, *Occhio dello spirito*

Captions

Unless specified otherwise, all photos are by Giuseppe Terragni, taken between 1941 and 1942 in Yugoslavia and in Russia (Source Terragni/Como Archives).

1 — p. 12
Cover of issue 153 of *L'Architettura. Cronache e storia*; monographic issue dedicated to Giuseppe Terragni and edited by Bruno Zevi, July 1968.

2, 3 — p. 14
Rendered image of the Casa del Fascio, Rome, created by CE·S·A·R - Centro Studi Architettura Razionalista with Flavio Mangione, Luca Ribichini and Attilio Terragni (published in *Terragni e Roma*, Prospettive Edizioni, Rome, 2015).

4 — p. 18
Photo of the newly built Casa Giuliani-Frigerio with wartime vegetable plots (Terragni/Como Archives).

5 — p. 20
Giuseppe Terragni, photomontage of Casa Giuliani-Frigerio and Cremona Cathedral (Terragni/Como Archives).

6 — p. 24
Giuseppe Terragni, view of Casa Vietti in Como (Terragni/Como Archives).

9, 10 — p. 30
Rendered image of Italian Glassworkers Union pavilion in Rome (UVI) created by CE·S·A·R - Centro Studi Architettura Razionalista with Flavio Mangione, Luca Ribichini and Attilio Terragni (published in *Terragni e Roma*, prospettive edizioni, Rome, 2015).

37 — p. 96
Front of postcard sent by Giuseppe Terragni to Luigi Zuccoli from Bucarest in October 1942 (Terragni/Como Archives).

38 — p. 96
Rear of postcard sent by Giuseppe Terragni to Luigi Zuccoli in 1942 (Terragni/Como Archives).

42 — p. 104
Photo of Giuseppe Terragni on his return to Italy in 1943 (Terragni/Como Archives).

44, 45 — p. 112
Sketches by Giuseppe Terragni drawn in Pavia (March/June 1943, Terragni/Como Archives).

46, 47 — p. 114
Giuseppe Terragni, perspective drawing for Cathedral, June/July 1943 (Terragni/Como Archives). Piero della Francesca, *Polyptych of the Misericordia* (detail), Museo Civico di Sansepolcro .

49 — p. 123
Photo of Giuseppe Terragni during transfer towards the Russian Front, summer 1941 (Terragni/Como Archives).

This volume was printed in
October 2020 by Tap Grafiche,
Poggibonsi (SI)